MÁIRTÍN Ó DIREÁIN

Selected Poems · Tacar Dánta

MÁIRTÍN Ó DIREÁIN

Selected Poems · Tacar Dánta

Selected and translated by

TOMÁS MAC SÍOMÓIN
DOUGLAS SEALY

THE GOLDSMITH PRESS
Ireland 1984

ACKNOWLEDGMENTS

We acknowledge the assistance of the Arts Council, An Chomhairle Ealaíon, in the production of this book.

For permission to reprint the Irish texts of the poems, we make grateful acknowledgement to An Clóchomhar Teo.

Published by The Goldsmith Press, Newbridge, Co. Kildare, Ireland.

CONTENTS

INTRODUCTION

The appearance of the collected poems of Máirtín Ó Direáin in 1980, hot on the heels of his eighth book of verse, was an event without precedent; no other poet in Irish has seen his collected work in print in his own lifetime. The publication was a tribute not only to the importance of what he had written, but also to his staying power and to the extent of his output. More than any of his contemporaries he has had an influence on younger poets and his dedication to his craft has given an example that will not be easy to follow. His work, traditional in many of its attitudes, themes and perceptions, original in its techniques and individualism, marks the watershed between the old and the new in Irish poetry.

Collections of poetry in Irish used to be divided into sections under headings such as Patriotism, Love, Elegy, Satire, Piety, Nature and Exile. This division seems quaint and artificial nowadays when a poem, whatever its subject matter, is expected to hint at multiple concerns, to suggest a whole world as seen from a private rather than a public point of view. Nevertheless, it would not be difficult to arrange the poems of Máirtín Ó Direáin under similar headings. Thus we find that about forty of the two hundred and fifty poems that comprise his *Dánta 1939-1979* (*Poems 1939-1979*) could come under the heading of Exile, for they express nostalgia for the Aran Islands and their way of life; thirty-five deal with the predicament of poet and poetry in contemporary Society; thirty-two deal with the theme of Love, and there are thirty Satires, in the Irish sense of a blistering attack on the enemy, in which traitors to the national ideals, 'ant-people' (modern mass man), and 'eunuchs' (bureaucrats, clerks, the non-creative) are excoriated. A smaller though significant grouping of the poems falls under the heading of Patriotism, and there are about a dozen poems which concentrate on evoking the innocence of Childhood and which show that, even in the Aran Islands, the author's remote and isolated birthplace, 'shades of the prison house begin to close upon the growing boy'. *Dánta 1939-1979* also contains eight Elegies as such, representing a minimal assimilation on the part of Ó Direáin to this aspect of the traditional poet's role, though we should qualify this by saying that the elegiac mood informs the most significant elements of his work.

These categories are neither exhaustive nor exclusive, but they do serve to show the particular importance of the theme of Exile in the work as a whole. The accidents of Ó Direáin's personal history have turned him into that representative figure of our time, the displaced person. The displacement is multiple: Ó Direáin is an islandman who has had to move to the mainland, a countryman who has been forced to live in urban surroundings, an Irish speaker who has earned his daily bread by working with English speakers, and an idealist in an age of materialism, always comparing the dignity of the past with the squalor of the present. A poet adrift in a world of prose, he has, like the Vietnamese boat people, been unable to adapt to an alien world and has remained aloof, at home nowhere except in the discomfort of his own mind.

Máirtín Ó Direáin was born in November 1910 in the townland of Sruthán, which lies near the western end of Inish-more, the largest of the Aran Islands. He was the eldest of four children and might have continued as his father before him, scraping a living from twenty acres of poor land, but his father died in 1917 and the resulting economic circumstances of his family made his subsequent exile inevitable. We may note that he was a monoglot Irish speaker until his middle teens and thence, given the environment in which he was reared, a product of Gaelic civilization to the utmost extent that this was possible in the Ireland of his time. This relationship with the Irish language was to make him unique among major Irish poets of the twentieth century. In January 1928 he left home and crossed the sea to Galway where he commenced working in the Central Post Office. In 1937 he moved to Dublin and worked in the Department of Education and, for a period, as Registrar of the National College of Art. An interest in writing manifested itself at this time. He had tried his hand at writing prose — to no great effect, in his own view — but he had never written any poetry before, nor indeed read very much of it, in either Irish or English.

A lecture he attended by chance in 1938 roused his dormant feeling for poetry and in 1942 he published the pamphlet *Coinnle Geala* (*Bright Candles*) and another in 1943, *Dánta Aniar* (*Poems from the West*), both at his own expense. These were small editions of about three hundred copies and many of them remained unsold. A number of the poems expressed, as might be expected, an overwhelming nostalgia for the Aran of his youth, but what was not to be expected was that he had discarded the traditional forms that he had grown up with, the songs with their long lines, regular rhythms and patterns of assonances, and had turned to short lines of varied length, rhythmical to be sure, but only loosely held together by an irregular use of assonance. Ó Direáin had been to some extent anticipated by Séamas Ó hAodha (1886-1967), who had made tentative experiments with free forms in his *Caoineadh na Mná* (*The Woman's Lamentation*) written in the 1930s, but not only was Ó hAodha's subject matter closely based on an extract from the diaries of the country schoolmaster Amhlaoibh Ó Súileabháin (1780-1838) but the form did not stray far from the improvised lamentations of the oral tradition. Ó Direáin's two little books, though very far from the emotional complexities, the startling use of imagery and the jarring syntax of what might be called modernism, did manifest a much freer and more experimental approach to the problems of writing poetry than had yet been seen in Irish.

Perhaps the most representative poem of those early collections is *Faoiseamh a Gheobhadsa* (*I Will Find Solace*) (page 2) where the form is so loose that the poem almost seems to have been constructed by adding line to line. The only thing Gaelic about this poem is its overall structure. The Scottish Gaelic poet and critic Derick Thomson (Ruaraidh Mac Thòmais) has remarked on a tendency in some Gaelic poetry to make the stanza rather than the poem the important unit. 'Such poems', he says, 'may consist of a series of stanzaic statements, e.g. about a chief or a clan. Each one is complete in itself . . . The unity of the poem becomes a purely thematic one, of a somewhat external sort: all the stanzas concern the same man or the same clan. But it would not harm this unity if some of the stanzas were missing, or if they came to us in the wrong order.' Raftery's *Cill Aodáin* is a case in point. And in *Faoiseamh a Gheobhadsa* the loosely connected chain of phrases (arbitrarily brought to an end by the last line of the verse, which acts as a refrain) are welded into a poem by the 'somewhat external' nostalgia of the islander for his island. Nevertheless the poem expresses a genuine feeling, and the construction, though loose, is not unmemorable.

The two early pamphlets may not quite have disappeared

without a trace but it was not until 1949, with the publication of a Selected Poems — *Rogha Dánta* — by the Irish language publishing firm of Sáirséal agus Dill that Máirtín Ó Direáin made an impact on the reading public. This was a handsome little book with a portrait drawing and three lino-cuts by Nano Reid, and was printed in a 'limited edition of 1200 copies' signed by the author. That this act of faith on the part of the publisher Seán Sáirséal Ó hÉigeartaigh was a great stimulus to his art, the poet himself acknowledges. Ten poems were preserved from the early pamphlets and fourteen hitherto uncollected poems made up the rest of the volume. About half a dozen poems from this book have become deservedly popular, and not only because they have become set as prescribed texts for various exams. Their simple heartfelt feeling, their nostalgia for a primal Eden, and their evocation of a traditional Gaelic life made a strong appeal to the older generation.

Parenthetically, it may be remarked that the printing of a poem as a school text is not without its perils, as Ó Direáin has related:

'I was in hospital a couple of years ago for an operation and a couple of nurses were looking after me as I lay on the trolley outside the theatre. One of them said to me: "Your poems are on the Leaving Cert., aren't they?" "Yes," said I. "A first cousin of mine failed her Leaving over one of your poems and now we have you where we want you. We could easily cut your throat!"' (In nti 7).

The best of these uncollected poems — possibly the one that threw the nurse's first cousin — was *Stoite* (*Uprooted*) (page 12). It is the first explicit statement of the conflict between urban and rural mores that was to be the inspiration of much of his best poetry. The nostalgia is still there — but braced by contempt, all the more bitter because it is self-contempt.

With the publication of *Ó Mórna agus Dánta Eile* (*Ó Mórna and Other Poems*) in 1957 Ó Direáin attained his full stature as a poet. In an interesting preface he modestly suggests that he was merely a mouthpiece for the poetry that lay all about him, in the natural surroundings of the island and more particularly in the speech of his people. J. M. Synge gave voice to the same sentiment, ·if more grandiloquently, in the preface to *The Playboy of the Western World* where he says: 'in countries where the imagination of the people, and the language they use, is rich and living, it is possible for a writer to be rich and copious in his words, and at the same time to give the reality, which is the root of all poetry, in a comprehensive and natural form . . .'

Like Synge, who had listened through a chink in the floor to the servant girls' chatter, Ó Direáin had always listened eagerly to the talk around him, but by 1957 he had been exiled from his native Aran, where Irish was in the very air he breathed, for nearly thirty years, and the Irish-speaking circles of Dublin could have provided only a threadbare substitute for the Irish he knew as a child. *Ó Mórna agus Dánta Eile* is the product of a deliberate strategy of evocation coloured by the experience of city life and marked by a growing cynicism. The language has expanded — as Ó Direáin's preface states: 'the speech a poet has heard in his youth is inadequate to express in verse every thought that his mind turns into images'. As well as the turns of speech garnered in Aran, Ó Direáin's poems now contain reflections of the Bardic poetry of the thirteenth to the sixteenth centuries, of the work of such seventeenth-century poets as Pádraigín Haicéad and Dáibhí Ó Bruadair, and of Bedell's Irish Bible (1685). Bedell's Bible is a constant companion of the poet, but not more so than that astonishing compendium of Irish word-lore and culture, Dineen's Irish-English Dictionary, in the new edition of 1934. His gleanings from the latter have been extensive. The influence of Yeats is now detectable, as well as that of Shakespeare; and the conception of *Ó Mórna*, the hero of the title poem of the collection, owes much to Ó Direáin's interest in the works of Nietzsche.

The difference between the earlier Ó Direáin and the poet who has arrived at his majority is, in many ways, the difference between *Faoiseamh a Gheobhadsa* and the outstanding *Cranna Fortil (Stout Oars)* (page 54) from *Ó Mórna*, a poem that no one else could have written. On the one hand — simplicity, easy accessibility; on the other — a complex weave of literary allusion, word play, and reference to a multiplicity of affective and experiential levels beneath the seemingly simple surface of the poem. *Cranna Foirtil* is basically about the realization that for the poet there can in the end be nothing as important as his 'craft or sullen art'. In its five short stanzas it brings together a number of the poet's pre-occupations — his search for certainty, his backward look towards a prelapsarian world, his respect for traditional ways — and it makes use of some of his favourite symbols — the tree for strength and stability, the redshank for the solitary artist, and the coal of fire for the artist's inspiration.

Some of the varied sources of Ó Direáin's language are exemplified by this poem. *Tamhanrud* (a thing as sturdy as a tree trunk) is a coinage of his own; *giolla gan chaithir* (a youth still without post-pubertal down or body hair) is an obsolete term from the older literature, which the poet found in Dineen's Dictionary; his use of *éadáil* and *guth* echoes a line from one of the great traditional songs:

Is ann a fuair mé guth gan éadáil is focal trom ó lucht an bhiadáin . . .

('Twas there I got profitless reproach and a heavy word from the backbiters . . .)

and the phrase *caipín an tsonais* (*the lucky cap*) refers to the widespread folk-belief that the possessor of a caul could never be drowned; the *ríocht dhorcha* (*the dark realm*) may be a local phrase but here it refers specifically to the pre-natal world from which such lucky caps emerge.

An unusual feature of the poem, in the context of Ó Direáin's work is the prominence given to local *pisreogs* or superstitions, perhaps rituals might be a better word. The twigs, the tongs, the patch of cloth and the iron bar, which the mothers of Aran used to place around the cradle, in order to protect the infant left alone in the house from evil spirits or misfortune, are enumerated neither credulously nor dismissively, and the poet has made these apparently insignificant memories into the heart of the poem. The old rituals are a symbol of a stable and continuing social order which the poet values, but which cannot protect him in his poetic career. The presence of these *pisreogs* in *Cranna Foirtil* shows the poet at his most unguarded and perhaps at his most honest.

Máirtín Ó Direáin has told us that the twilight ambience of some of the poetry of *Ó Mórna agus Dánta Eile* and of *Ár Ré Dhearóil* (*Our Wretched Era*), published in 1962, owes much to his readings of Oswald Spengler, the German philosopher of History, whose bleak vision of the future of Western Civilisation must have been congenial to a poet increasingly disposed to see himself as the last voice of a doomed culture. A similar disenchantment is evident in much of the work of T. S. Eliot, and it is interesting to compare parts of *Ár Ré Dhearóil*, the title poems of the collection (page 66), with this chorus from Eliot's *The Rock*:

The river flows, the seasons turn,
The sparrow and the starling have no time to waste.
If men do not build
How shall they live?
When the field is tilled
And the wheat is bread
They shall not die in a shortened bed
And a narrow sheet . . .

And yet the composition of *Ár Ré Dhearóil* predates Ó Direáin's acquaintanceship with the poetry of T. S. Eliot. Even a cursory study of the literature of Europe will reveal that the poetic *Zeitgeist* can and does overlap in diverse tongues; clearly, great care must be exercised in postulating literary influences.

Just as Yeats needed his Phases of the Moon and Eliot his mystical apprehension of the still point of the turning world, so Ó Direáin has needed his *oileán rúin*, his secret island, not only as symbol but also as a yardstick against which to measure the fallings off of life.

A major part of the attraction of *Ó Mórna agus Dánta Eile* and subsequent 'island' poems is the way the island now wavers between being a symbol and being a real island. Thus, without losing any of its particularity, Inishmore may stand for the innocence and guilelessness of youth posited against the deviousness of age or for an enduring value standing rock-solid against the ravages of urban rootlessness. Or, again, it may be a symbol of the unbroken Gaelic tradition and a living reproach to its urbanised and anglicised successor.

After a fellow-poet, Seán Ó Ríordáin, had written of his admiration for Ó Direáin's poetry, 'a poetry sprung from unceasing pondering on a little island in the sea, on Christmas candles, on a woman's love', the poet responded in the poem *Ionracas* (*Guilelessness, Integrity, Truth*):

Coinneod féin an t-oileán
Seal eile i mo dhán

Toisc a ionraice atá
Cloch, carraig is trá.

(I will keep the island/A little longer in my poem/Because of the truth of/Stone, rock and strand.)

The imaginative identification of Aran with a standard of behaviour that would be impossible to attain is a transcendence of the nostalgia noted earlier, but the extreme romanticism of the gesture cannot be denied, linked as it is with the suggestion that the inhabitants of Aran, despite their only too human failings, have absorbed this honesty from the spartan rigour of their circumstances. The poem *Gleic Mo Dhaoine* (*My People's Struggle*) from *Ó Mórna agus Dánta Eile* makes this point:

Dúshlán na ndúl a spreag a ndúshlán . . .
Slíodóireacht níor chabhair i gcoinne na toinne,
Ná seifteanna caola i gcoinne na gcloch úd . . .

(The challenge of the elements prompted their challenge . . .
Opportunism was no help against the wave,
Nor subtle ploys against those stones . . .)

In this and many other poems the poet is clearly filled with the envy of the sedentary man for the man of action and is disposed to see the islander's struggle for existence as inevitably heroic. It could be said of Ó Direáin as it has been said of J. M. Synge:

> He noted only those aspects of island life which fed his own imagination and supported his views . . . while he referred to the hardness of the islander's life he did so rather with the admiration of the romantic than with the concern of the sociologist . . . Haunted by thoughts of mortality, he saw in the endless battle of the islanders with the elements and their constant nearness to sudden death a parable of the human condition . . . in their ancient culture, their stories and mythic understanding of the natural world, he perceived a kind of knowledge that lay deeper than that of intellect . . . (Robin Skelton: *J. M. Synge and his World*, 1971).

That passage does not by any means define the whole of Ó
Direáin's sensibility, but taken in conjunction with the title poem
of *Ó Mórna agus Dánta Eile* and with the poet's aversion
towards many features of contemporary life, it helps to show
how close he had come to the attitudes expressed in Yeats's
poetic testament:

Irish poets, learn your trade,
Sing whatever is well made,
Scorn the sort now growing up
All out of shape from toe to top,
Their unremembering hearts and heads
Base-born products of base beds.
Sing the peasantry, and then
Hard-riding country gentlemen,
The holiness of monks, and after
Porter-drinkers' randy laughter;
Sing the lords and ladies gay
That were beaten into the clay
Through seven heroic centuries;
Cast your mind on other days
That we in coming days may be
Still the indomitable Irishry.

The long poem *Ó Mórna* is based on the life of one of the
hereditary landlords of Aran. In Ó Direáin's book of prose
sketches, *Feamainn Bhealtaine* (*May Seaweed*), he mentions
how the landlord's cattle were driven over a cliff at the time of
the Land League and how the islanders had to pay compen-
sation. This awoke Ó Direáin's interest in the man and the land-
lord class he belonged to and it is with no little surprise that we
read the poem about him. Instead of an attack it is an apologia
— the landlord's arrogant and tyrannical treatment of his
tenants is, if not pardoned, at any rate excused. The eponymous
hero is a thug and a bully, but he is treated with sympathy and
even admiration, for he was a proud and passionate man; Ó
Direáin's dislike and contempt is reserved for the philistines, the
opportunists, the apathetic, the scurrying lilliputians of the
metropolis, the *seangánfhir* or ant-people.
    The primacy assigned to 'will' and 'passion' in the philosophy
of Friedrich Nietzsche no doubt encouraged the poet in his

portrait of a 'hard-riding country gentleman' but the creation of Ó Mórna as an alter ego enabled the poet to give expression to what can only be described as a glorification of the male sexual drive. Sex is treated gingerly in the other poems, cf. *Agallamh* (*Dialogue*) (page 76); only in this one poem has the moral censor that lives in the minds of so many Irish people, and not just of the religious, relaxed its grip. *Ó Mórna* is not as explicit as Merriman's *Cúirt an Mheán Oíche* (*The Midnight Court*) and it lacks the latter's humour and fluency, but it is with *Cúirt an Mheán Oíche* that *Ó Mórna* is best compared. There is a similar energy at work in both poems, a similar exhilaration at the breaking of taboos, but the poet Ó Direáin takes his pleasures seriously and Ó Mórna is a Don Juan figure, doomed only to be satiated, never satisfied.

Ó Mórna is not only a Don Juan, he is also a member of the landlord class, a petty king in his own domain who appears in the poem to have regarded himself as 'Beyond Good and Evil'. The poet's admiration for him was probably reinforced by his admiration for Yeats and the prominent role of the Anglo-Irish — most of them of the landlord class — in Irish cultural affairs including, most importantly, the promotion of the Irish language. And in one of his poems, *Gabhair* (*Goat*) he suggests:

> . . . *gur mhó ag an seandream*
> *Faoin seanreacht féin an náire*
> *Ná an dream a chuaigh in airde.*

> (. . . *that the old crowd*
> *Even under the old dispensation had more sense of honour*
> *Than the crowd that gained ascendancy.*)

And yet, Ó Direáin has written poems such as *An Stailc* (*The Strike*) (page 48), *Séamas Ó Conghaile* (*James Connolly*) (page 129), *De Dheascaibh an Úis* (*Because of Usury*) (page 60) etc. in which the plight of the working class and of the underdog is stated with clarity and force. There is only an apparent contradiction here. The Irish psyche has yet to recover completely from the distortion caused by centuries of economic and cultural domination — the beaten Irish maintained an ambivalent attitude towards their Anglo-Irish overlords: a sullen vengefulness co-existing with an almost hysterical need to imitate the 'quality' (the very designation is significant). Ó Direáin's poetry faithfully mirrors this ambivalence and its cloak of servility and also insists that we reconsider the only too easily dismissed contribution of the Anglo-Irish to our present nation-state.

In *Ár Ré Dhearóil* (1962) 'island poems' are less frequent than in any of his previous collections and the state of the nation and the people who now surround him becomes the more immediate object of his poetic attention. And what he sees fills him with anger and despair, expressed in poems such as *Na Coillteáin* (*The Eunuchs*) (page 86), in which the censors of his (Ó Direáin's) work are lambasted. *Éire ina bhfuil Romhainn* (*To Ireland in the Coming Times*) (page 96), in which Caitlín Ní hUalláchain ꞌ becomes a whore, and *Mar Chaitheamar an Choinneal* (*How We Wasted the Candle*) (page 98), in which blame for the botching of the Irish revolution is assigned. Ó Direáin sees the followers of the 'holy' cause of Irish independence as being in themselves holy and the image of the consecrated host occurs three times in this collection, as for example in *Mothú Feirge* (*Feeling of Anger*):

Feic a mhic mar a chreimid na lucha
An abhlann a thit as lámha na dtréan
Is feic fós gach coileán go dranntach
I bhfeighil a chnáimh ina chró bréan
Is coinnigh a mhic do sheile agat féin.

(*See, boy, how the mice nibble/The Host that fell from the hands of the brave/And see also each snarling cur/Guarding its bone in its foul lair/And keep your spittle to yourself, boy.*)

'The abomination of desolation', as Coventry Patmore wrote, 'is always in the holy places' and Ó Direáin's image barely contains his rage and resentment.

Much of *Cloch Choirnéil* (*Corner Stone*) (1962) is taken up with similar concerns and also contains a group of poems that deal with the subject of love. These are modelled directly on the courtly poetry of the fourteenth to seventeenth centuries, written by such as Piaras Feiritéir, an aristocrat of Norman descent who took part in the rising of 1641, and was hanged in 1653. Thus, for example, the opening line of one of Feiritéir's most famous poems: *'Leig díot t'airm, a mhacaoimh mná'* (*Lay aside thy arms, maiden)* reappears, slightly changed, in *Cloch Choirnéil* as *Leag uait na hAirm (Lay the arms aside)*.

The comparatively intricate forms of this poetry provided Ó Direáin with an established form for the expression of love and a technical challenge to which he responded with all the ingenuity of a bardic *ollamh*. Nevertheless, these poems, of all the poet's work, are apt to prove the least satisfying to modern readers. 'They have little psychology . . . and, for the most part, conceive women with an enviable simplicity, as beautiful and false.' These words of Robin Flower about the Irish poetry of courtly love apply with equal force to the love poems of Ó Direáin. As the contemporary love poem is expected to be confessional, self-revelatory and, above all, expressive of the complexity of sexual love at the intellectual, affective and physical levels, Ó Direáin's essays in the Courtly Style prove much less congruent with our present sensibility than his poems of exile and alienation, which strike a ready chord in the modern breast. An age, it seems, needs its own poetic voice to speak its own truth.

The most significant poem in *Cloch Choirnéil* is *Berkeley* (page 106). Boswell's anecdote is well known — 'After we came out of church we stood talking for some time together of Bishop Berkeley's ingenious sophistry to prove the non-existence of matter, and that everything in the Universe is merely ideal. I observed that though we are satisfied his doctrine is not true, it is impossible to refute it. I shall never forget the alacrity with which Johnson answered, striking his foot with mighty force against a large stone, till he rebounded from it, "I refute it thus!"' The 'ideal' is what is contained in the mind and Ó Direáin is coming to realise that his island, the island as he saw it, had no existence outside his own mind and he must have begun to wonder if he had ever given a true picture of it.

This could have been a fruitful perception, but the weakening of Ó Direáin's governing myth left him floundering for direction and his last two books, *Crainn is Cáirde (Trees and Friends)* (1970) and *Ceacht an Éin (The Bird's Lesson)* (1979), though not without their felicities, contain few poems that match the resonance and appeal of the earlier 'island poems'. Some depend too exclusively on traditional phrase or custom, and others repeat what had already been said better before. Nevertheless, there are key poems in these two books. In *Ualach (Burden)* (page 110) from *Crainn is Cáirde* the poet, moving in the course of the poem from the stately to the sardonic, aligns himself with one of the greatest of his predecessors: and in *Ceacht an Éin*, in the poem entitled *Neamhionraic Gach Beo* (*(The Essence is not in the Living)* (page 120) the poet, having discovered in *Berkeley* that the 'island' was only a construction of the mind, seems to have come to the conclusion that the real island, the nucleus around which his ideal island had formed, is a reduction of the island of his youth to a congeries of inanimate matter: *'cloch carraig is trá'* (*stone, rock and strand)*). In this mood of despair he feels compelled to dismiss the warmth of human association as *neamhionraic* (*impure, not of the essence*) and only recognises *ionracas* (*purity, integrity*) in two ancient portraits. This extraordinary bitterness is directed at himself and his poetry. The island, he says, has left his poem; its dead but pure integrity can have nothing to do with the impurity of life as seen by the poet. *Neamhionraic Gach Beo* may not be one of Ó Direáin's best poems but it is more revealing than many of his successes. Only a deep and growing dissatisfaction with his creative work could have occasioned it.

That poem has needed some discussion because it is by no means easy of access but another poem in this volume, the noble elegy on Máirtín Ó Cadhain, tells, with directness, how this integrity was once embodied in a living man. It is the finest of all the patriotic poems.

The poetic career of Ó Direáin has been remarkable by any standards, but especially in view of the well-nigh moribund state of Irish poetry when he first came to it. This career spanned the post-war period, when the dreams of Pearse and Connolly were still regarded by many as practicable ideals, the Lemass era, and its aftermath — the media-dominated consumer society of the Eighties. Ó Direáin has observed, with dismay, the transformation of a primarily agrarian society into a primarily urban one, the attenuation of traditional values, the rejection of the political and cultural ideals that sustained those who fought for an independent Ireland and, most of all, the creeping disappearance of the Irish language itself, the very medium of his art. Such fundamental and far-reaching change has not occurred without causing its share of psychological trauma, without making strangers in their own land of those whose allegiance is to the older vision.

Máirtín Ó Direáin, by virtue of his background and sensibility, is uniquely qualified to speak for such 'strangers' and the most enduring part of his poetry gives vivid expression to the anger and pain attendant on this state of internal exile which he suffered and continues to suffer. Indeed the following verse from his poem *O'Casey* (from *Cloch Choirnéil*), in which he mourns the death in England of the exiled dramatist Seán O'Casey, could have been a description of himself:

A lán dár fhigh tú as cnámhghoin
Níorbh áil le h-ál an tsámhrith;
Ós deoraí cheana fear na cnise
Ba dheoraí faoi dhó thusa.

(Much of what you wove from the wound in the bone/Was not pleasant in the ears of that sleek brood;/Since the artist is already an exile/You were an exile twice over.)

Ó Direáin is the only poet of our time who has worn the mantle of Ó Bruadair, Ó Rathaile and the other great sixteenth- and seventeenth-century poets who inveighed against the forces that would consign their art to oblivion. His work, at its best, is the poetic response of the Gael in our present day to the Anglo-American culture that threatens to still his voice for ever. From a more prosaic angle, it is the human face of the mass of statistics that quantify the great demographic changes of the last fifty years and, as such, mandatory reading for all who would know Ireland.

Our choice of fifty-one poems from a total of over 250 has been governed by the wish not only to show the poet at his best, but also to make the selection as representative as possible. This has led to conflict at times, and poems that are better, arguably, than many we have included in this collection have been omitted. The reader may note a dearth of love poems here; we have already given some reasons for this to which we might add that their particular effects depend so much on the resources of the Irish language as to make them untranslatable. Our selection may seem to some to place too heavy an emphasis on *Ó Mórna agus Dánta Eile* and *Ár Ré Dhearóil*; this emphasis stems from our conviction that these collections represent the high water mark of Ó Direáin's achievement and the clearest and most forceful exposition of themes that have continued to exercise his talent ever since.

Poetry cannot be fully translated and we find ourselves close to the position of Robert Lowell who, in his introduction to *Imitations* said: 'Boris Pasternak has said that the usual reliable translator gets the literal meaning but misses the tone, and that in poetry tone is of course everything. I have been reckless with literal meaning, and laboured hard to get the tone. Most often this has been *a* tone, for *the* tone is something that will always more or less escape transference to another language and cultural moment. I have tried to write live English and to do what my authors might have done if they were writing their poems now and in America.' In this spirit, initially, we prepared somewhat free versions which we felt might stand in their own right as English poems while conveying the tone, if not the exact letter, of the original. However, our awareness that many readers will have a modicum of Irish, and that a more literal rendering affords better access to the originals, caused us to modify these versions and make them as far as possible a line by line translation, if not completely word for word — which would certainly be unreadable. Our surgery was drastic for all that and we would caution the English monoglot reader that all too often for our liking beauty has had to be sacrificed to fidelity.

Is mar chomhartha ómóis do Mháirtín, is mar mhór-chomhartha buíochais dó as a bhfuil déanta aige ar son Éigse na Gaeilge, a thugamar aghaidh ar an saothar seo i gcéaduair. Ní cloch ar bith a chaith an fathach seo ar an gcarn ach carraig. Ach mholfadh muid don léitheoir focla Lowell thuas a mheabhrú agus gan a bheith taobh le na haistriúcháin seo amháin más uaidh filíocht an Direánaigh a mheas go críochnúil is go beacht. Is i nGaeilge na mbunleagan amháin atá éirim agus croí shaothar Uí Dhireáin ar fáil agus is i gclé na teanga úd a chaith-eanns an fiosróir a bheith, le gabháil 'ar an domhain' seachas 'fanúint le cladach'. Baineann an scéal céanna, mórán, le saothúlacht agus litríocht na hÉireann fré chéile aniar go dtí lár na haoise seo caite, agus le mórán dár cumadh ó shoin.

Tá muid fíorbhuíoch do Mháirtín as an gcomhairle is an spreagadh a thug se dúinn fhad's bhí an obair seo idir lámha againn. Tá sé thar am ag cliú an fhile seo paor a thógáil 'thar chríocha aithnid', dar linn, agus dá gcuirfeadh an chnuasacht seo teannadh leis an mbóithreoireacht seo níor mhiste sin.

TOMÁS MAC SÍOMÓIN DOUGLAS SEALY
Lá na Féile Bríde 1984

xxi

Selected Poems · Tacar Dánta

FAOISEAMH A GHEOBHADSA

Faoiseamh a gheobhadsa
Seal beag gairid
I measc mo dhaoine
Ar oileán mara,
Ag siúl cois cladaigh
Maidin is tráthnóna
Ó Luan go Satharn
    Thiar ag baile.

Faoiseamh a gheobhadsa
Seal beag gairid
I measc mo dhaoine,
Ó chrá croí,
Ó bhuairt aigne,
Ó uaigneas duairc,
Ó chaint ghontach,
    Thiar ag baile.

I WILL FIND SOLACE

I will find solace
For a short time only
Among my people
On a sea-girt island,
Walking the shore
Morning and evening
Monday to Saturday
    In my western homeland.

I will find solace
For a short time only
Among my people,
From what vexes the heart,
From a troubled mind,
From soured solitude,
From wounding talk,
    In my western homeland.

DÍNIT AN BHRÓIN

Nochtaíodh domsa tráth
Dínit mhór an bhróin,
Ar fheiceáil dom beirt bhan
Ag siúl amach ó shlua
I bhfeisteas caointe dubh
Gan focal astu beirt:
D'imigh an dínit leo
Ón slua callánach mór.

Bhí freastalán istigh
Ó línéar ar an ród,
Fuadar faoi gach n-aon,
Gleo ann is caint ard;
Ach an bheirt a bhí ina dtost,
A shiúil amach leo féin
I bhfeisteas caointe dubh,
D'imigh an dínit leo.

GRIEF'S DIGNITY

I once had a glimpse
Of grief's great dignity
When I saw two women
Emerge from a crowd
In dark funereal garb
Neither uttering a word:
Dignity departed with them
From the large and noisy crowd.

A tender was in
From a liner in the roadstead,
Everyone was scurrying around,
Hubbub and loud chatter;
But the silent couple
Who emerged on their own
In dark funereal garb
Dignity departed with them.

CUIMHNÍ CINN

Maireann a gcuimhne fós i m'aigne:
Báiníní bána is léinte geala,
Léinte gorma is veistí glasa,
Treabhsair is dráir de bhréidín baile
Bhíodh ar fheara cásacha aosta
Ag triall ar an Aifreann maidin Domhnaigh
De shiúl cos ar aistear fhada,
A mhúsclaíodh i m'óige smaointe ionamsa
Ar ghlaine, ar úire, is fós ar bheannaíocht.

Maireann a gcuimhne fós i m'aigne:
Cótaí cóirithe fada dearga,
Cótaí gorma le plúirín daite,
Seálta troma aníos as Gaillimh,
Bhíodh ar mhná pioctha néata
Ag triall ar an Aifreann mar an gcéanna;
Is cé go bhfuilid ag imeacht as faisean,
Maireann a gcuimhne fós i m'aigne
Is mairfidh cinnte go dté mé i dtalamh.

MEMORIES

Their memory lives on in my mind:
White bawneen coats and gleaming shirts,
Blue shirts and grey waistcoats,
Trousers and drawers of homespun tweed
That old and honoured men used to wear
As they went to Mass on Sunday morning
Making the long journey by foot,
When I was young they turned my thoughts
To purity, freshness, and also to piety.

Their memory lives on in my mind:
Long stately skirts coloured crimson,
Blue skirts that were dyed with indigo,
Heavy shawls down from Galway,
That neat and well-dressed women used to wear
As they went to Mass in the selfsame manner;
And though they're rapidly going out of fashion
Their memory lives on in my mind
And will still live on till I go to the graveyard.

CUIREADH DO MHUIRE

An eol duit, a Mhuire,
Cá rachair i mbliana
Ag iarraidh foscaidh
Do do Leanbh Naofa,
Tráth a bhfuil gach doras
Dúnta Ina éadan
Ag fuath is uabhar
An chine dhaonna?

Deonaigh glacadh
Le cuireadh uaimse
Go hoileán mara
San Iarthar cianda:
Beidh coinnle geala
I ngach fuinneog lasta
Is tine mhóna
Ar theallach adhainte.

Nollaig 1942

8

INVITATION TO THE VIRGIN

Dost thou know, O Mary,
Where thou wilt go this year
Seeking shelter
For thy Holy Child,
When every door
Is closed in His face
By the hate and pride
Of the human race?

Deign to accept
My invitation
To a sea-bound island
In the remote West:
Shining candles will be
Lit in each window
And a fire of turf
On each hearthstone kindled.

Christmas 1942

RÚN NA mBAN

Tráthnóna Domhnaigh ab ionduala
Ansiúd iad cois tine,
Na mná agus na seálta
Casta ar a gcloigne,
Bhíodh tae ann i gcónaí
Ar ócáid den chineál,
Is braon ag dul thart de
Ó dhuine go duine.

Thosaíodh an chaint
An broideadh is an sioscadh,
Uille ar ghlúin ag cur leis na focla;
D'ordaítí mise amach ar na bóithre,
Gan a bheith istigh ag slogadh gach focail,
Go mba folláine amuigh mé
Ar nós mo leithéid eile.

D'imínn sa deireadh,
M'aghaidh lasta is mé gonta
Ach is mairg nach bhfanainn:
Nuair a smaoiním anois air
Cá bhfíos cén rúndiamhair
Nach eol d'aon fhear beirthe
A phiocfainn ó mhná
Scartha thart ar thine,
Iad ag ól tae
Is seálta ar a gcloigne?

THE WOMEN'S SECRET

Nearly every Sunday evening
There they were by the fire,
The women with their shawls
Wrapped about their heads.
There was always tea
On such occasions,
And they passed a sup around
From one to another.

The talk started,
The nudge and the whisper,
Elbow on knee emphasizing the words;
I used to be ordered out on the roads,
Not to be inside wolfing each word,
I'd be healthier out in the air
Like the rest of the lads.

I left in the end,
Blushing and hurt
But I wish I had stayed:
When I think of it now
Who knows what secret lore
Unknown to any man alive
I'd have snatched from the women
Ranged round a fire,
Drinking tea
With their shawls on their heads?

STOITE

Ár n-aithreacha bhíodh,
Is a n-aithreacha siúd,
In achrann leis an saol
Ag coraíocht leis an gcarraig loim.

Aiteas orthu bhíodh
Tráth ab eol dóibh
Féile chaoin na húire,
Is díocas orthu bhíodh
Ag baint ceart
De neart na ndúl.

Thóg an fear seo teach
Is an fear úd
Clai nó fál
A mhair ina dhiaidh
Is a choinnigh a chuimhne buan.

Sinne a gclann,
Is clann a gclainne,
Dúinn is éigean
Cónaí a dhéanamh
In árais ó dhaoine
A leagfadh cíos
Ar an mbraon anuas.

Beidh cuimhne orainn go fóill:
Beidh carnán trodán
Faoi ualach deannaigh
Inár ndiaidh in Oifig Stáit.

UPROOTED

Our fathers
And their fathers before them
Were at grips with life
And wrestled with the naked rock.

They were happy
When the seasons revealed to them
Earth's kindly abundance
And they were eager
To hold their own
Against the force of the elements.

One man built a house
And another
A dyke or a wall
Which outlived him
And kept his name alive.

We, their children,
And their children's children,
Are compelled
To make our homes
In apartments whose owners
Would levy rent
On the drip from the ceiling.

We will be remembered yet:
A stack of files
Weighed down with dust
Will survive in a government office.

AN tEARRACH THIAR

Fear ag glanadh cré
De ghimseán spáide
Sa gciúnas séimh
I mbrothall lae:
 Binn an fhuaim
 San Earrach thiar.

Fear ag caitheamh
Cliabh dá dhroim,
Is an fheamainn dhearg
Ag lonrú
I dtaitneamh gréine
Ar dhuirling bhán:
 Niamhrach an radharc
 San Earrach thiar.

Mná i locháin
In íochtar díthrá,
A gcótaí craptha,
Scáilí thíos fúthu:
 Támhradharc sítheach
 San Earrach thiar.

Tollbhuillí fanna
Ag maidí rámha,
Currach lán éisc
Ag teacht chun cladaigh
Ar órmhuir mhall
In ndeireadh lae:
 San Earrach thiar.

14

SPRING IN THE WEST

A man scraping clay
From the tread of a spade
In the serene calm
On a warm day:
    The sound is sweet
    During Spring in the west.

A man throwing
A creel off his back,
And the red seaweed
Glittering
In the sunshine
On a white stone beach:
    A vivid sight
    During Spring in the west.

Women in the shallows
At furthest ebb
With their skirts tucked up
And reflections beneath them:
    A tranquil sight
    During Spring in the west.

Faint hollow strokes
Of oars,
A currach full of fish
Approaching the shore
On a slow gold sea
At day's end:
    During Spring in the west.

ÁRAINN 1947

Feadail san oíche
Mar dhíon ar uaigneas,
Mar fhál idir croí is aigne
Ar bhuairt seal,
Ag giorrú an bhealaigh
Abhaile ó chuartaíocht,
An tráth seo thiar
    Níor chualas.

Amhrán aerach,
Scaradh oíche is lae,
Ó ghroífhear súgach,
Gaisce ard is goití dúshláin
Is gach uaill mhaíte
Ag scoilteadh clár an chiúnais,
Tráth a mbíodh gníomha gaile a shinsear
Á n-aithris do dhúile an uaignis,
An tráth seo thiar
    Níor chualas.

Liú áthais ná aitis
Ó chroí na hóige
Ag caitheamh 'cloch neart'
Mar ba dhual tráthnóna Domhnaigh,
Nó ag cur liathróid san aer
Le fuinneamh an bhuailte,
An tráth seo thiar
    Níor chualas.

Ní don óige feasta
An sceirdoileán cúng úd.

ARAN 1947

Whistling at night
As a defence against the eeriness,
A barrier between heart and brain
In a time of disquiet,
Shortening the road
Home from late visiting,
This time in the West
I heard not.

A lively song,
When day left night behind,
From a tipsy stalwart,
Loud boasts and defiant gestures
And many an arrogant yell
Splitting the length of the silence
While the brave deeds of their forefathers
Were named to the spirits of solitude,
This time in the West
I heard not.

A shout of joy or pleasure
From the heart of the young
As they tossed the great stone,
Their Sunday evening custom,
Or shot a ball in the air
With force behind the stroke,
This time in the West
I heard not.

Not for the young any more,
That narrow windswept island.

MAITH DHOM

I m'aonar dom aréir,
I mo shuí cois mara,
An spéir ar ghannchuid néal
Is muir is tír faoi chalm,
Do chumraíocht ríonda
A scáiligh ar scáileán m'aigne
Cé loinnir deiridh mo ghrá duit
Gur shíleas bheith in éag le fada.

Ghlaos d'ainm go ceanúil
Mar ba ghnách liomsa tamall,
Is tháinig scread scáfar
Ó éan uaigneach cladaigh;
Maith dhom murarbh áil leat
Fiú do scáil dhil i m' aice,
Ach bhí an spéir ar ghannchuid néal
Is muir is tír faoi chalm.

FORGIVE ME

Last night, being alone,
Sitting beside the sea,
Few clouds were in the sky
And land and sea were calm,
The shadow of your beauty
Was cast on the screen of my mind,
The last flicker of my love for you
That I thought dead this long time.

I fondly called your name
As I used to once,
And I heard a frightened screech
From a lonely bird on the shore;
Forgive me if you did not wish
Even your dear shade to come near me,
But few clouds were in the sky
And land and sea were calm.

Ó MÓRNA

A ródaí fáin as tír isteach
A dhearcann tuama thuas ar aill,
A dhearcann armas is mana,
A dhearcann scríbhinn is leac,
Ná fág an reilig cois cuain
Gan tuairisc an fhir a bheith leat.

Cathal Mór Mac Rónáin an fear,
Mhic Choinn Mhic Chonáin Uí Mhórna,
Ná bí i dtaobh le comhrá cáich,
Ná le fíor na croise á ghearradh
Ar bhaithis chaillí mar theist an fhir
A chuaigh in uaigh sa gcill sin.

Ná daor an marbh d'éis cogar
    ban,
D'éis lide a thit idir uille
Is glúin ar theallach na sean,
Gan a phór is a chró do mheas,
A chéim, a réim, an t-am do mhair,
Is guais a shóirt ar an uaigneas.

Meas fós dúchas an mhairbh féin
D'eascair ó Mhórna mór na n-éacht,
Meabhraigh a gcuala, a bhfaca sé,
Ar a chuairt nuair a d'éist go géar,
Meabhraigh fós nár ceileadh duais air,
Ach gur ghabh chuige gach ní de cheart.   ▶

Ó MÓRNA

Traveller straying in from the mainland,
You who gaze at a tomb on a cliff-top,
Who gaze at a coat of arms and a slogan,
Who gaze at inscription and flagstone,
Do not leave the graveyard by the bay
Before you know the dead man's story.

The man was Cathal Mór the son of Rónán,
Son of Conn son of Conán Ó Mórna,
But don't rely on common hearsay
Nor crone signing the cross on her forehead
To give you a true report of the man
Who entered the grave in that churchyard.

Don't condemn the dead man because of women's
    whispers,
Following a hint let fall between elbow
And knee by the old people's hearth,
Before you consider his blood and lineage,
His station, his power, the age he lived in,
And the snares that loneliness sets for his sort.

Consider also the dead man's heredity,
How he sprang from the line of great Ó Mórna,
Think of all he heard, all he saw,
As he went around he listened intently,
Remember also no prize was denied him
But all that he took was taken by right.   ▶

Chonaic níochán is ramhrú dá éis,
Chonaic mná ag úradh bréidín,
Gach cos nocht ó ghlúin go sáil
Ina slis ag tuargain an éadaigh,
Bean ar aghaidh mná eile thall
Ina suí suas san umar bréige.

Chonaic is bhreathnaigh gach slis ghléigeal,
Chonaic na hógmhná dá fhéachaint
Dá mheas, dá mheá, dá chrá in éineacht.
D'fhreagair fuil an fhireannaigh thréitheach,
Shiúil sí a chorp, las a éadan,
Bhrostaigh é go mear chun éilimh.

'Teann isteach leo mar a dhéanfadh fear,
Geallaimse dhuit go dteannfar leat,
Feasach iad cheana ar aon nós,
Nach cadar falamh gan géim tú,
Ach fear ded' chéim, ded' réim cheart.'
Pádhraicín báille a chan an méid sin.
Briolla gan rath! mairg a ghéill dó.

Iar ndul in éag don triath ceart
Rónán Mac Choinn Mhic Chonáin,
Ghabh Cathal chuige a chleacht,
A thriúcha is a chumhachta,
A mhaoir, a bháillí go dleathach,
A theideal do ghabh, is a ghlac.

An t-eolas a fuair sna botháin
Nuair a thaithigh iad roimh theacht i seilbh,
Mheabhraigh gach blúire riamh de,
Choigil is choinnigh é go beacht,
Chuaigh chun tairbhe dó ina dhiaidh sin
Nuair a leag ar na daoine a reacht.

▶

22

He saw the washing and then the thickening,
Saw the women scouring frieze,
Each naked leg from knee to heel
Like a wash-staff pounding the cloth,
Woman sitting opposite woman
Along the sides of the makeshift trough,

Saw and noted each white wash-staff,
Saw the young women gazing at him,
Sizing him up and tantalizing him.
The blood of the robust male responded,
Traversed his body, suffused his face
And urged him on to swift demand.

'Press in there close to them like a man,
I warrant you'll feel an answering pressure,
Sure they know already
You're no empty spunkless cod
But a man of your rank and direct ancestry.'
Pádhraicín the bailiff spoke those words.
A worthless rascal! You should have ignored him.

After the death of the titular lord,
Ronán the son of Conn the son of Conán,
The young Cathal took over his prerogative,
His lands and his jurisdictions,
His stewards and bailiffs as the law appointed,
He took his title and his power.

The knowledge gained in the cabins
Frequented before his accession,
He'd remembered every least bit of it,
Saved it up and treasured each detail;
He used it later for his own advantage
When he laid his law on the people.

▶

23

Mheabhraigh sé an té bhí uallach,
Nach ngéillfeadh go réidh dá bheart,
Mheabhraigh sé an té bhí cachtúil,
An té shléachtfadh dó go ceart,
Mheabhraigh fós gach duais iníonda
Dár shantaigh a mhian ainsrianta.

Mhair ár dtriath ag cian dá thuargain,
Ba fánach é ar oileán uaigneach,
Cara cáis thar achar mara
B'annamh a thagadh dá fhuascailt,
Is théadh ag fiach ar na craga
Ag tnúth le foras is fuaradh.

Comhairlíodh dó an pósadh a dhéanamh
Le bean a bhéarfadh dó mar oidhre
Fireannach dlisteanach céimeach
Ar phór Uí Mhórna na haibhse,
Seach bheith dá lua le Nuala an Leanna,
Peig na hAirde is Cáit an Ghleanna.

An bhean nuair a fuair Ó Mórna í
Níor rug aon mhac, aon oidhre ceart;
Níor luigh Ó Mórna léi ach seal,
Ba fuar leis í mar nuachair;
Ina cuilt shuain ní bhfuair a cheart,
É pósta is céasta go beacht.

Imíonn Ó Mórna arís le fuadar,
Thar chríocha dleathacha ag ruathradh,
Ag cartadh báin, ag cartadh loirg,
Ag treabhadh faoi dheabhadh le fórsa,
Ag réabadh comhlan na hóghachta,
Ag dul thar teorainn an phósta. ▶

He thought of the one who'd been stiffnecked,
Who wouldn't readily comply with his schemes,
He thought of the one who'd been obsequious,
The one who'd truly grovel before him,
He thought long of each virginal prize
For which he hankered with unbridled passion.

Our chief lived prey to melancholy's assaults,
Odd man out on a remote island,
An understanding friend from across the sound
Seldom came to his rescue
And he hunted on across the crags
Yearning for ease and alleviation.

He was advised to take in marriage
A woman who would bear him as heir
A legitimate and noble male-child
To continue the line of mighty Ó Mórna,
Instead of consorting with Alehouse Nuala,
Peg of Ard and Kate of Glen.

The wife, after Ó Mórna found her,
Bore him no son, no proper heir;
Ó Mórna lay with her only a while,
His newfound bride made a frigid mate;
In her drowsy bed his right was denied,
His marriage was nothing but torture.

Ó Mórna departs once more in haste,
Rampaging beyond the legal limits,
Digging the fallow land, digging the furrowed,
Ploughing with headlong violence,
Forcing the gate of virginity,
Crossing the bounds of marriage.   ▶

Ag réabadh móide is focail
Ag réabadh aithne is mionna,
A shúil thar a chuid gan chuibheas,
Ag éisteacht cogar na tola
A mhéadaigh fothram na fola,
Ina rabharta borb gan foras.

Ceasach mar mheasadh den chré lábúrtha
Leanadh Ó Mórna cleacht a dhúchais,
Thógadh paor thar chríocha aithnid,
Go críocha méithe, go críocha fairsing,
Dhéanadh lá saoire don subhachas
Dhéanadh lá saoire don rúpacht.

Maoir is báillí dó ag fónamh
Ag riaradh a thriúcha thar a cheann,
Ag comhalladh a gcumhachta níor shéimh,
Ag agairt danaide ar a lán,
An t-úll go léir acu dóibh féin
Is an cadhal ag gach truán.

Sloinnte na maor a bheirim díbh,
Wiggins, Robinson, Thomson, agus Ede,
Ceathrar cluanach nár choigil an mhísc,
A thóg an cíos, a dhíbir daoine,
A chuir an dílleacht as cró ar fán,
A d'fhág na táinte gan talamh gan trá.

Níor thúisce Ó Mórna ar ais
Ar an talamh dúchais tamall
Ná chleacht go mear gach beart
Dár tharraing míchlú cheana air:
Threabhadh arís an chré lábúrtha,
Bheireadh dúshlán cléir is tuata.

▶

26

Breaking pledge and word,
Breaking commandment and vow,
Prompted by his greed's excess,
Listening to the whisper of desire
Increasing the clamour of his blood
In its rich and restless springtide.

Sated, they said, of base-born flesh,
Ó Mórna followed the ways of his forebears,
Used to take jaunts from known domains
To lush domains, to vast domains,
Abandoning all for the sake of pleasure,
Abandoning all for the harlot's embrace.

Stewards and bailiffs were at his disposal,
Administering his territories on his behalf,
Cruelly carrying out his instructions,
Causing grievous loss to many;
They had the whole of the apple to themselves,
Each starveling had the peel.

I give you the names of the stewards,
Wiggins, Robinson, Thomson and Ede,
Four crafty men who shunned no evil,
Who collected rents, who evicted tenants,
Who drove the orphan away from his hovel,
Who left hundreds without field or strand.

No sooner had Ó Mórna been back
On his native ground for a while
Than he quickly got up to the same tricks
Which had already gained him disrepute;
He ploughed again the base-born flesh
In open defiance of priest and layman.   ▶

27

Tháinig lá ar mhuin a chapaill
Ar meisce faoi ualach óil,
Stad in aice trá Chill Cholmáin
Gur scaip ladhar den ór le spórt,
Truáin ag sciobadh gach sabhrain
Dár scaoil an triath ina dtreo.

Do gháir Ó Mórna is do bhéic,
Mairbh a fhualais sa reilig thuas
Ní foláir nó chuala an bhéic;
Dhearbhaigh fós le draothadh aithise
Go gcuirfeadh sabhran gan mhairg
In aghaidh gach míol ina n-ascaill.

Labhair an sagart air Dé Domhnaigh,
Bhagair is d'agair na cumhachta,
D'agair réabadh na hóghachta air,
Scannal a thréada d'agair le fórsa,
Ach ghluais Ó Mórna ina chóiste
De shodar sotail thar cill.

D'agair gach aon a dhíth is a fhoghail air,
D'agair an ógbhean díth a hóghachta air,
D'agair an mháthair fán a háil air,
D'agair an t-athair talamh is trá air,
D'agair an t-ógfhear éigean a ghrá air,
D'agair an fear éigean a mhná air.

Bhi gach lá ag tabhairt a lae leis,
Gach bliain ag tabhairt a leithéid féin léi,
Ó Mórna ag tarraingt chun boilg chun léithe
Chun cantail is seirbhe trína mheisce,
Ag roinnt an tsotail ar na maoir
Ach an chruimh ina chom níor chloígh.   ▶

28

One day he came on horseback,
Laden to the gills with drink,
Stopped beside the strand of Kilcolman
To scatter a handful of gold for sport;
The starvelings snatched at each sovereign
The lord tossed at their feet.

Ó Mórna roared and gave a shout,
The dead of his kin in the graveyard above
Must have heard that shout;
He declared as well with a sneer of contempt
That he could easily put up a sovereign
To match each louse in their arm-pits.

The priest named him on Sunday,
Threatened to use the powers against him,
Denounced him for profaning virginity,
Vehemently denounced the scandal to his flock,
But Ó Mórna set off in his coach
At an arrogant trot past the church.

Denounced by all for raiding and rapine,
Denounced by the girl for taking her maidenhead,
Denounced by the mother for her family scattered,
Denounced by the father for field and strand,
Denounced by the youth for raping his sweetheart,
Denounced by the husband for raping his wife.

Each day that passed meant one day less,
Each year that passed meant another gone,
Ó Mórna was falling to flesh and greyness,
More sour and petulant in his drunken bouts,
Venting his spleen on the stewards
But the worm in his flesh he could not defeat. ▸

Nuair a rug na blianta ar Ó Mórna,
Tháinig na pianta ar áit na mianta:
Luigh sé seal i dteach Chill Cholmáin,
Teach a shean i lár na coille,
Teach nár scairt na grásta air,
Teach go mb'annamh gáire ann.

Trí fichid do bhí is bliain le cois,
Nuair a cuireadh síos é i gCill na Manach
D'éis ola aithrí, paidir is Aifreann;
I measc a shean i gCill na Manach
I dteannta líon a fhualais,
Ar an tuama armas is mana.

An chruimh a chreim istigh san uaigh tú,
A Uí Mhórna mhóir, a thriath Chill Cholmáin,
Níorbh í cruimh do chumais ná cruimh d'uabhair
Ach cruimh gur cuma léi íseal ná uasal.
Go mba sámh do shuan sa tuama anocht
A Chathail Mhic Rónáin Mhic Choinn.

When the years caught up with Ó Mórna
The aches of desire were replaced by pain,
He lay for a while in the house of Kilcolman,
His ancestral house in the heart of the wood,
A house that grace had never shone on,
A house where laughter seldom sounded.

Threescore he was and a year besides
When he was buried in Cill na Manach
After Unction, Penance, prayer and Mass:
Among his ancestors in Cill na Manach
Along with the tally of his kin,
On the tomb a coat of arms and a slogan.

The worm that gnawed you in the grave,
Great Ó Mórna, lord of Kilcolman,
Was not the worm of your vigour nor of your hauteur
But a worm that heeds not birth nor blood.
Calm be your slumber in the tomb tonight,
Cathal, son of Ronán son of Conn.

FÍS AN DAILL

Bhí seanchaí ar m'aithne,
É liath agus dall,
A d'aithris an méid seo
Do scata gan aird:
'Bíonn longa faoi sheolta bána
Ar farraige thiar,
Is fós faoi shoilse geala'
Ar an seanchaí liath.
'Bíonn fir is mná ina gcéadta ar bord
Is iad gléasta go gléigeal'
Ar an seanchaí dall.
'Bíonn fíon is beoir is feoil le fáil
Is iad á roinnt ar chách go fial'
Ar an seanchaí liath.
Is chonaic mé an scata
Ina thimpeall ag magadh
Is dúirt duine amháin
Nach raibh ann ach dall
Is nach raibh ina chaint
Ach rámhaillí ard;
Is chonaic mé gné
An tseanchaí léith
Is í ar lasadh ag fís na háille,
Is d'éirigh mé faoi fheirg
Gur fhág mé an áit,
Is gur dhúras nárbh eisean
Ach iadsan a bhí dall.

THE BLIND MAN'S VISION

I knew a storyteller,
Grey-haired and blind,
Who recited these words
To a heedless throng:
'Ships with white sails
Cross the western sea,
Ablaze with lights'
Said the grey-haired storyteller.
'Hundreds of men and women on board,
All richly adorned'
Said the blind storyteller.
'There's plenty of wine and meat and ale
And a generous share is given to all'
Said the grey-haired storyteller.
And I saw the crowd
Around him mocking
And one man said
He was just a blind man
And that his talk was only
Raving nonsense.
And I saw the face
Of the grey-haired storyteller
Shining with visionary delight,
And I rose in anger
And left that place,
And said not he
But they were blind.

A FHAOILEÁIN UCHTBHÁIN

A fhaoileáin uchtbháin
Méanar duit mar táir,
Ar muin na mara glaise,
Is lonnaí laga gan chás
Ag déanamh láíocht
Le do bhrollach.

A fhaoileáin uchtbháin
Déan malairt liom fiú lá,
Go gcuirfead díom crá
Ar bharr na toinne,
Go mbeidh lonnaí laga gan chás
Ag déanamh láíocht
Le mo bhrollach.

WHITE-BREASTED GULL

White-breasted gull,
Fortunate your fate,
Riding the green swell,
While soft careless ripples
Press gently
Against your breast.

White-breasted gull,
Take my place for a day,
Till I shed my sorrow
Afloat on the wave,
And soft careless ripples
Press gently
Against my breast.

DEIREADH RÉ

Fir na scéal mo léan!
Is an bás á leagadh,
Mná na seál á leanacht
Is mise fós ar marthain
I measc na bplód gan ainm,
Gan 'Cé dhár díobh é' ar a mbéal
Ná fios mo shloinne acu.

Ní háil liom feasta dar m'anam
Dáimh a bhrú ar chlocha glasa!
Ní fáilteach romham an charraig,
Mé ar thóir m'óige ar bealach,
Mé i m'Oisín ar na craga,
Is fós ar fud an chladaigh,
Mé ag caoineadh slua na marbh.

END OF AN ERA

I grieve for the tellers of tales!
Death lays them low;
The shawled women follow
While I live on
Among the nameless crowds;
'Who is he?' doesn't spring to their lips,
My name to them unknown.

I no longer wish, by my soul,
To force friendship on grey stones!
The rock does not welcome me
As I seek my youth on the road,
And I am Oisín on the crags
And wandering on the strand
Making lamentation for the hosts of the dead.

CUIMHNE AN DOMHNAIGH

Chím grian an Domhnaigh ag taitneamh
Anuas ar ghnúis an talaimh
San oileán rúin tráthnóna;
Mórchuid cloch is gannchuid cré
Sin é teist an sceirdoileáin,
Dúthaigh dhearóil mo dhaoine.

Chím mar chaith an chloch gach fear,
Mar lioc ina cló féin é,
Is chím an dream a thréig go héag
Cloch is cré is dúthaigh dhearóil,
Is chímse fós gach máthair faoi chás
Ag ceapadh a háil le dán a cuimhne.

A SUNDAY MEMORY

I see the sun of Sunday shining
Down on the contours of the land
In the dear island this afternoon;
Wealth of stones and dearth of clay
Are the signature of the rugged island,
The bleak ancestral land of my people.

I see how the stone has abraded each man,
How it has crushed him into its own shape,
And I see the throng that deserted till death
Stone and clay and bleak ancestral land,
And I see as well each grief-struck mother
Securing her children with memory's noose.

ÓMÓS DO JOHN MILLINGTON SYNGE

An toisc a thug tú chun mo dhaoine
Ón gcéin mhéith don charraig gharbh
Ba chéile léi an chré bheo
Is an leid a scéith as léan is danaid.

Níor éistis scéal na gcloch,
Bhí éacht i scéal an teallaigh,
Níor spéis leat leac ná cill,
Ní thig éamh as an gcré mharbh.

Do dhuinigh Deirdre romhat sa ród
Is curach Naoise do chas Ceann Gainimh,
D'imigh Deirdre is Naoise leo
Is chaith Peigín le Seáinín aithis.

An leabhar ba ghnáth i do dhóid
As ar chuiris bréithre ar marthain;
Ghabh Deirdre, Naoise is Peigín cló
Is thug léim ghaisce de na leathanaigh.

Tá cleacht mo dhaoine ag meath,
Ní cabhair feasta an tonn mar fhalla,
Ach go dtaga Coill Chuain go hInis Meáin
Beidh na bréithre a chnuasaís tráth
Ar marthain fós i dteanga eachtrann.

HOMAGE TO JOHN MILLINGTON SYNGE

The impulse that brought you to my people
From the distant pasture to the harsh rock
Was partnered by the living clay
And the intimations of loss and sorrow.

You didn't listen to the tale of the stones,
Greatness lived in the tale of the hearth,
You paid no heed to tombstone or graveyard,
No whimper escapes the lifeless dust.

Deirdre appeared before you on the road
And Naoise's currach weathered Ceann Gainimh;
Deirdre and Naoise went to their death
And Pegeen flung abuse at Shawneen.

The book was always in your hand —
You brought the words in it to life;
Deirdre, Naoise and Pegeen took form
And leaped like heroes from the pages.

The ways of my people decay.
The sea no longer serves as a wall.
But till Coill Chuain comes to Inis Meáin
The words you gathered then
Will live on in an alien tongue.

TEAMPALL AN CHEATHRAIR ÁLAINN

A fhothraigh chrín!
A chill an rúin!
Cérbh iad an ceathrar naomh?
An ceathrar álainn úd,
Atá sínte faoi do bhinn?

Ní feas do neach
Cérbh as do thriall
Ná fáth a dteacht ó chéin
Ach gur cheathrar iad
A char an Briathar,
Cuing an Chrábhaidh
Is buarach Dé.

Ní dán dóibh feasta
Tráth ná clog,
Ó leagadar díobh
A gcarcair choil,
Nuair a thiomnaigh siad
Don chré a gcorp,
Is a n-anam do Rí na nGrást.

Tá buannacht ag Dia
Ar an áit ó shin,
Is A shíocháin mar chochall
Thart ar an mball,
Is ní scéithfir a rún,
A fhothraigh chrín.

THE CHURCH OF THE FOUR BEAUTIFUL ONES

You crumbling ruin!
You church of mystery!
Who were the four saints?
The four beautiful ones
Who lie beneath your gable?

No one knows
Where they came from
Or why they left some distant place,
But they were four
Who loved the Word,
Piety's yoke
And the halter of God.

They need heed no longer
Office or bell,
Since they discarded
Their souls' prison,
When they dedicated
Their bodies to the clay
And their souls to the King of Grace.

God has claimed
The ground ever since
And His peace like a veil
Encloses the place,
And you will not betray their secret,
You crumbling ruin.

AN tÓINMHID

Chuaigh óinmhid thart ar fud an Aonaigh
Ag agairt an tslua is á ngríosadh,
D'agair gach aon de chlann an chúraim
Is dúirt leo go léir le dúthracht:
'Scaoil d'Éan chun na Gréine,
Scaoil d'Éan chun na Gréine.'
Níor thuig an slua an agairt,
Níor thuig ach caint an mhargaidh,
Níor thuig ach reic is ceannach,
Do ghlac leis an óinmhid fearg,
Do shaighid an daoscar garg
A mhairbh ar an láthair é;
Ach tháinig Aingeal i lár an Aonaigh
A d'ardaigh a anam go láthair an Tiarna,
File, Fáidh, is Naomh in aon
As géibheann na gnáthaíochta saor.

THE BUFFOON

A buffoon went round the fair
Pleading with the people and prompting them,
He pleaded with each of the merchant clan
And said to them all with fervour:
'Let your bird soar to the sun!
Let your bird soar to the sun!'
The throng knew not the sense of his plea,
Knew only market cant,
Knew only bargain and barter,
Grew furious with the buffoon,
Incited the ire of the rabble
Who killed him on the spot.
But an angel descended in the midst of the fair
And raised his soul to a place by the Lord.
Poet, prophet and saint in one
Free from convention's fetters.

TEAGHLACH ÉINNE

Fóill, a ghaineamh, fóill!
Fearann tearmainn, seachain!
Cosc do ghnó mall,
Do ghnó foighdeach fág,
Is téadh Cill Mhic Chonaill slán.

Éanna Mac Chonaill Dheirg
Triath Oirialla ba oirearc,
Do thogh an áit mar ionad
Mar scoil léinn don iomad
A chuir a cáil thar críocha.

Fóill, a ghaineamh, fóill!
Stad is lig don bhall,
Fág binn, stua, is doras;
Ní cuibhe ar shaothar Mhic Chonaill
Brat an dearmaid ar deireadh.

ÉANNA'S COMMUNITY

Wait, sand, wait!
Avoid this place of sanctuary!
Halt your slow task,
Your patient work must cease
And Mac Conaill's church be spared.

Éanna, Red Conall's son,
Illustrious Chief of Oriel once,
Chose this place to found
A learned school for the many
Who spread its fame abroad.

Wait, sand, wait!
Stop and leave this place alone,
Spare gable, arch and doorway;
Mac Conaill's toil does not deserve
The mantle of final oblivion.

AN STAILC

Scilling bhreise an focal faire!
Ó bhéal na mbocht, ó chlann an duig,
Scilling a dhiúltaigh na toicí móra,
Scilling bhreise san uair do na fir,
'Ne'er a wing, ne'er a wet.'

Scilling an focal, scilling an déirce
A tharraing ar na toicí racht na mbocht,
Na cruimhe á gcreimeadh thíos faoi na fóda
Á ghuidhe dóibh arís le fórsa,
'Ne'er a wing, ne'er a wet.'

Droim le balla ag caoineadh an tuillimh,
Ag agairt na hainnise ar an sotal,
Scilling an focal, scilling an t-éileamh,
Bia, deoch, cíos is éadach,
'Ne'er a wing, ne'er a wet.'

Scilling á hiarraidh, beart is daonna
Ná codáin á ríomadh mar éileamh,
Á ríomhadh ar chaoi nach léir dom,
Fios a d'fhionnas ó chlann an duig,
'Ne'er a wing, ne'er a wet.'

THE STRIKE

An extra shilling is the watchword!
In the mouths of the poor, the men of the docks,
A shilling refused by the wealthy owners,
An extra shilling an hour for the men,
'Ne'er a wing, ne'er a wet.'

Shilling was the word, a beggarly shilling
That drew down on the rich the wrath of the poor;
May maggots gnaw them below the sod
Was the poor man's venomous supplication,
'Ne'er a wing, ne'er a wet.'

With backs to the wall they complain of their wages,
Confronting arrogance with their miserable plight,
The word's a shilling, the claim is a shilling,
Food and drink, rent and clothing,
'Ne'er a wing, ne'er a wet.'

To ask for a shilling's a more human action
Than computing fractions to support the claim,
And counting them up in a way I know not,
That's what I learned from the men of the docks,
'Ne'er a wing, ne'er a wet.'

NA TURAIS

Oíche Fhéile Sin Seáin
Is tinte cnámh in éag,
Bheiridís leo fir is mná
Gach duine a phluid féin,
Thugadh aghaidh ar chill,
Ar thobar, ar leaba naoimh,
Is thugadh cion an ghnáis
I bpáirt do Dhia.

Gan Ord, gan Aifreann
Gan riar na cléire,
Thar thobar beannaithe,
Thar atharla is leaba,
Thar chinnleac, thar charn,
Chaitheadh dáil na bpeacach
Ag bréagadh na bhflaitheas
Ó oíche go maidin.

THE PILGRIMAGES

On St. John's Eve
As the bonfires died,
Men and women carried
A blanket each,
Walked the old graveyards,
The wells, the saint's beds
And paid custom's tribute
Together to God.

Without mass or service
Or priest's dispensation,
By holy well,
Burial place and bed,
By headstone and cairn
The sinner's meeting assembled,
Entreating heaven
From night till morning.

LEIGHEAS NA hEAGLA

An cuimhin libhse an malrach
A ghoin sibh go deacrach,
Tráth ar chuir sibh thart scéal
Is nath ó dhuine go duine
Is m'athair ag fanacht
Lena chónra chláir uaibh?

Murar cuimhin fós, a fheara,
Ní thógaim oraibh feasta é,
Is gur fadó a dáileadh
Libh féin an chré dhubh,
Is go dtuigim le sealad
Nach bhfuil leigheas ar an eagla
Ach scéal, is nath, is gáire.

SALVE FOR FEAR

Do you remember the youth
You wounded to the quick
When you passed tale
And quip from man to man
And my father waiting
For his coffin from your hands?

Even if you don't remember, men,
I no longer blame you
For long ago you were committed
To the dark earth
And I have known for some time now
That the only salve for fear
Is story, quip and laughter.

CRANNA FOIRTIL

Coinnigh do thalamh a anam liom,
Coigil chugat gach tamhanrud,
Is ná bí mar ghiolla gan chaithir
I ndiaidh na gcarad nár fhóin duit.

Minic a dhearcais ladhrán trá
Ar charraig fhliuch go huaigneach;
Mura bhfuair éadáil ón toinn
Ní bhfuair guth ina héagmais.

Níor thugais ó do ríocht dhorcha
Caipín an tsonais ar do cheann,
Ach cuireadh cranna cosanta
Go teann thar do chliabhán cláir.

Cranna caillte a cuireadh tharat;
Tlú iarainn os do chionn,
Ball éadaigh d'athar taobh leat
Is bior sa tine thíos.

Luigh ar do chranna foirtil
I gcoinne mallmhuir is díthrá,
Coigil aithinne d'aislinge,
Scaradh léi is éag duit.

STOUT OARS

Stand your ground, my soul;
Cleave to every rooted stock;
Don't behave like a callow youth
When your false friends depart.

You've often seen a redshank
Alone on a wet rock;
Though he drew no wealth from the wave
His lapse incurred no censure.

From your dark realm you brought
No lucky caul around your head
But the ritual wands were placed
To protect you in your cradle.

Useless sticks were placed around you;
An iron tongs above,
Beside you a piece of your father's clothing,
A poker placed in the fire.

Lean on your own stout oars
Against neap-tide and ebb,
Keep alight the coal of your vision;
To part with that is death.

OLC LIOM

A thuistí a tháinig romham sall
Go dtí Dónall an tSrutháin,
Olc liom mar tháscaim díbhse,
Nár chuireas is nár bhaineas
Is nár thógas fós fál,
Nach ndearna mac chun fónaimh
Dár bpór, dár nós, dár ndúchas.

Táir agam gach giota páir
Mar luach, mar dhuais nuair a fhaighim,
Ar shaothar suarach gan cháil,
Seach bhur ngleic le toinn aird,
Le cré in éadan carraige,
Ag rámhadh in aghaidh bhur ndáin
Ar ucht ard na farraige.

REMORSE

Fathers who came before me
Back to Donall of Sruthán
I regret to have to inform you
That I have neither sown nor harvested
Nor even built a wall,
Nor made a son to carry on
Our line, our ways, our heritage.

I despise each paper scrap,
The wage and recompense I get
For petty meaningless labour,
Unlike your fight with the towering wave,
With clay against the rock,
Rowing in defiance of fate
On the high breast of the ocean.

SIC TRANSIT ...

Clann Mhic Thaidhg, na flatha
Faoi raibh na hoileáin thiar
Cúig céad bliain go léir,
Síol Bhriain na n-éacht,
An pór teann tréan,
Cá bhfuil a nead cré?

Na flatha a bhris a réim,
A choinnigh a gcion féin
Den talamh garbh gann
Ceithre céad bliain dá n-éis,
Gheobhair i reilig thuas ar aill
Leaba a bhfualais is a nead.

Cois cuain atá a bhfeart
Láimh le trá na gceann,
Ar an tuama tá armas greanta
Is mana ar leacht in airde,
Mana a bheireann dúshlán Flaitheartach:
Fortuna favit fortibus —
Ach tá meirg ag creimeadh an ráille.

Tá meirg ag comhrá le seanchóiste
I gclós an tí mhóir le seal anall,
Níl lua ar na flatha ná tuairisc
I dteach a sean ná i gCill Cholmáin,
Ó chuaigh an Flaitheartach deiridh síos
Le líon a fhualais san uaigh láimh le trá.

SIC TRANSIT . . .

Clann Mhic Thaidhg, the lords
Who ruled the western islands
For all of five hundred years,
Offspring of the great Brian,
That strong firm stock,
Where is their nest of clay?

The lords who broke their sway,
Who kept their own parcel
Of the rough scanty soil
For the next four hundred years,
In a graveyard upon a cliff you'll find
The bed and nest of their kin.

Their burial ground is by the bay
Beside the Strand of the Heads,
A coat of arms is carved on the tomb
And a slogan on the slab above,
A slogan that bears the O'Flahertys' challenge:
Fortuna favit fortibus —
But rust is gnawing at the rail.

Rust is talking with an old coach
In the yard of the big house still,
No one mentions the lords or their fame
In their ancestral home nor in Kilcolman
Since the last O'Flaherty went to join
The rest of his kin in the grave beside the strand.

DE DHEASCA AN ÚIS ...

De dheasca an úis:
    Ní le neach teach ná dídean,
    Talamh, trá, ná gabháltas dílis,
    Capall, buaibh, ní leis ná caora,
    Ní leis a anam ná a chroí ceart.

De dheasca an úis:
    Gach modarphlé idir daoine,
    Gach foghail, gach díth, gach fána,
    Tá an ógh ag reic a náire
    I gcoim na hoíche ag fairdeal.

De dheasca an úis:
    Is iomaí créatúr gan díleas
    Ach a bhfuil uime ina éadach,
    Tá mílte ina mogha ag éigean
    Is an síol calctha i mbléin na tíre.

De dheasca an úis:
    Tá meirg ar chéachtaí,
    Báid ag lobhadh i nduga tréigthe,
    Daoine ag dorchú ar a chéile,
    An cian gabhalscartha ar chéadta.

De dheasca an úis:
    Tá an ghin sa mbroinn
    I ngeall don léan dubh,
    Is tuilleadh a ghinfí
    Gan ghineadh in aonchor.

BECAUSE OF USURY

Because of usury:
    None owns house or shelter,
    Land, strand or inherited holding,
    None owns horse or cows or sheep,
    None owns soul or heart by right.

Because of usury:
    Each shady deal among people,
    Each theft, each loss, each downfall,
    The virgin hawking her shame
    Astray in the heart of night.

Because of usury:
    Many creatures have no property
    Except for the clothes on their backs,
    Need has slaves by the thousand
    And the seed has clogged in the loins
        of the land.

Because of usury:
    Rust forms on ploughs,
    Boats rot at abandoned jetties,
    Darkness veils the people's speech,
    Gloom sits astride the masses.

Because of usury:
    The embryo in the womb
    Is mortgaged to grief
    And more that should have been born
    Will not be born at all.

CUID CAIDÉISE

Cuid caidéise tusa a bhean
Sa teach mór i lár na coille
(Tearc a shórt ar fhód teallaigh)
Is ní fios do neach cén borradh,
Cén cumasc tola is fola
Idir dhá cheann na hEorpa
A chuaigh do chumadh do chlósa.

Inis dom, ós gnó dom é
Fios an ghalair úd a chur
Ar breodh de na slóite,
Céard faoi deara d'aghaidhse
Bheith rite is do shnó mar atá?
An é nach ndófar go deo
Aon Traoi i do chomhair?

An é gur fada uait
Coill Chuain is an té bhí leat?
Cá bhfios fós nach tú an bhean?
Ach tabhair do chúl don allód feasta,
Tá cinn chomhluchta beo is mótair leo!
Is dá dtagadh Naoise féin an treo,
B'fhéidir nach mbeadh mar a thuairisc.

CURIOSITY

You arouse curiosity, woman,
In the great house among the trees
(There are few like it on mensal lands)
And nobody knows what turmoil,
What mingling of blood and will
Between the two poles of Europe
Went to mould your shape.

Tell me — for it is my profession
To diagnose the sickness
That struck so many down —
What force made your face so drawn
Though your skin retains its bloom?
Is it that no one will ever burn
A Troy for you?

Can it be that you are pining
For Coill Chuain and the man who was yours?
Who can say for certain you're not the woman?
But turn away now from all that's passed,
Directors are astir in company cars!
And Naoise himself, if he should come this way,
Might not be all he's cracked up to be.

CRAINN OÍCHE SHEACA

Géag-uaigneach gach crann
Scartha leis an uile,
Íbirtchrot gach crann anocht
I bhfianaise na cruinne
Is é a dhínit a loime.

Samhail a bheirim do gach crann
Páischrann an chéasta,
Fíor ar gach crann a chím,
Géagscartha clíréabtha
Tréigthe ag an duine.

TREES ON A FROSTY NIGHT

Bare-branched each tree
Cut off from the universe,
Each tree like a victim tonight,
The round world in witness,
Its nakedness is its exaltation.

I imagine each tree
Is the passion-tree of the crucifixion,
I see a figure on each tree,
Spreadeagled and pierced in the side,
Abandoned by man.

ÁR RÉ DHEARÓIL

Tá cime romham
Tá cime i mo dhiaidh,
Is mé féin ina lár
I mo chime mar chách,
Ó d'fhágamar slán
Ag talamh, ag trá,
Gur thit orainn
Crann an éigin.

Cár imigh an aoibh,
An gáire is an gnaoi,
An t-aiteas úrchruthach naíonda?
Gan súil le glóir,
Le héacht inár dtreo
Ná breith ar a nóin ag éinne.

Níl a ghiodán ag neach
Le romhar ó cheart,
Níl éan ag ceol
Ar chraobh dó,
Ná sruthán ag crónán
Go caoin dó.

Tá cime romham
Tá cime i mo dhiaidh,
Is mé féin ina lár
I mo chime mar chách,
Is ó d'fhágamar slán
Ag talamh, ag trá
Bíodh ár n-aird
Ar an Life chianda. ▶

OUR WRETCHED ERA

A prisoner before me
A prisoner behind,
I stand between
A prisoner like all,
Since we said goodbye
To field, to strand,
Since we bent under
Necessity's yoke.

Where has cheerfulness gone,
The laughter and the liking,
The spontaneous child-like joy?
No hope of renown,
No scope for valour
And none has time for the evening prayer.

None has his plot
To dig of right,
No bird is singing
To him from a branch
Nor stream murmuring
Gently to him.

A prisoner before me,
A prisoner behind,
I stand between
A prisoner like all,
And since we said goodbye
To field, to strand,
Let us turn our minds
To the ancient Liffey.

▶

Bíodh ár n-aire
Ar an abhainn
Ar an óruisce lán
A chuireann slán
Le grian deiridh nóna.

Bímis umhal ina láthair
Is i láthair an tsrutha
Is samhail den bheatha
Ach gur buaine,
Mar is samhail an abhainn
De shráid an tslua
Ach gur uaisle.

An lá is ionann ag mná
Faiche is sráid,
Páirc, trá, is grianán,
Ná bíodh cime gnáis
Gann faoi dhearbhdhíona:

Tá fairsinge díobh ann
Mar luaim thíos i mo dhiaidh iad,
Is deirid lucht cáis
Nach bhfuilid gan bhrí leo —

An macha cúil
Tráthnóna Sathairn,
An cluiche peile,
An imirt chártaí
Is ósta na bhfear
Ina múchtar cásamh.　▶

Let us turn our attention
To the river
To the brimming golden water
That bids farewell
To the late evening sun.

Let us be humble in its presence
And in the presence of the moving water,
A symbol of life
But more enduring,
For the river is an image
Of the crowded street
But more sublime.

When women make no distinction
Between greensward and street
Meadow, strand and summer-house,
Let not the prisoner of convention
Be short of asylums:

There are plenty of them,
I list them below
And the compassionate say
They have their uses —

The back-garden
On Saturday evening,
The game of football,
The session at cards,
And the men's bar
Where complaint is quenched.   ▶

Crot a athar thalmhaí
Do shúil ghrinn is léir,
Ag teacht ar gach fear
Atá i meán a laethe,
A chneadaíonn a shlí chun suíocháin
I mbus tar éis a dhinnéir.

Ní luaifear ar ball leo
Teach ná áras sinsir,
Is cré a muintire
Ní dháilfear síos leo,
Ach sna céadta comhad
Beidh lorg pinn leo.

Is a liacht fear acu
A chuaigh ag roinnt na gaoise
Ar fud páir is meamraim,
Ag lua an fhasaigh,
An ailt, an achta.

Is a liacht fear fós
A thug comhad leis abhaile,
Is cúram an chomhaid
In áit chéile chun leapa.

Is mná go leor
A thriall ina n-aice
Ar thóir an tsó,
An áilleagáin intrigh;
Galar a n-óghachta
A chuaigh in ainseal orthu
A thochrais go dóite
Abhras cantail.

▶

70

The gait of his rural father
Can be seen by a sharp eye,
Overtaking each man
In middle-age
As he sighs his way to a seat
In the after-dinner bus.

Soon no one will trace them
To house or ancestral mansion,
And to the earth of their kin
They will not be committed,
But hundreds of files
Will bear the mark of their pen.

So many men among them
Dissipated their talents
On paper and parchment,
Citing the precedent,
Paragraph, decree.

And so many other men
Took a folder home with them
And the care of the folder
To their wifeless bed.

And many women
Journeyed beside them
In quest of luxury,
The merry-go-round;
The disease of their virginity
Turned chronic
And they bitterly wound
A fretful thread.

▶

Mná eile fós
Ba indúilmheara ag feara,
Ba féile faoi chomaoin
Ba ghainne faoi chairéis,
A roinn a gcuid go fairsing
I ngéaga an fhir
Ba luaithe chucu
Ar chuairt amhaille,
Ar scáth an ghrá
Nár ghrá in aon chor
Ach aithris mhagaidh air,
Gan ualach dá éis
Ach ualach masmais.

Na hainmhithe is na héin
Nuair a fhaighid a gcuid dá chéile,
Ní gach ceann is luaithe chucu
A ghlacaid in aon chor.

I gcúiteamh an tsíl
Nach ndeachaigh ina gcré,
I gcúiteamh na gine
Nár fhás faoina mbroinn,
Nár iompair trí ráithe
Faoina gcom,
Séard is lú mar dhuais acu
Seal le teanga iasachta
Seal leis an ealaín,
Seal ag taisteal
Críocha aineola,
Ag cur cártaí abhaile
As Ostend is Paris,
Gan eachtra dála
Ar feadh a gcuarta,
Ná ríog ina dtreo
Ach ríog na fuaire.

72 ▶

Yet other women
Most alluring to men,
Most generous in bestowal,
Most niggard of scruple,
Lavished their all
In the arms of the man
Who first approached them
On a sly visit,
On the pretext of love
That wasn't love at all
But a mocking counterfeit,
With no consequent burden
But a burden of loathing.

Birds and beasts
When they couple together,
The firstcomer's not always the one
They decide to take.

To compensate for the seed
That did not enter their flesh,
To compensate for the child
That did not grow in their womb,
That they didn't carry nine months
In the hollow of their bodies,
The least they'd accept as dowry
Was a spell at foreign languages,
A spell at the arts,
A spell touring
In foreign parts,
Sending home postcards
From Ostend and Paris,
Without one loving encounter
In all their journeys,
Knowing no grip
But the grip of apathy.

▶

Tá cime romham
Tá cime i mo dhiaidh,
Is mé féin ina lár
I mo chime mar chách,
Is a Dhia mhóir
Fóir ar na céadta againn,
Ó d'fhágamar slán
Ag talamh ag trá,
Tóg de láimh sinn
Idir fheara is mhná
Sa chathair fhallsa
Óir is sinn atá ciontach
I bhásta na beatha,
Is é cnámh ár seisce
An cnámh gealaí
Atá ar crochadh thuas
I dtrá ár bhfuaire
Mar bhagairt.

A prisoner before me
A prisoner behind,
I stand between them
A prisoner like all,
And Almighty God
Succour the hundreds of us
Since we said goodbye
To field, to strand,
Take us by the hand
Both men and women
In the deceitful city
For we are the guilty ones
Wasting life —
The bone of our sterility
Is the bone moon
That hangs above
In the strand of our apathy
As a portent.

AGALLAMH

A dúirt an chiall:
Bí ann i ngan fhios
Do na cíocha crochta,
D'airm na cluana,
Do dhiamhair na suirí,
Don chorp seang,
Don fholt leabhair.
A dúirt an croí:
Cá bhfuil mo dheachú
Go héag na hola?

A dúirt an chiall:
Suigh ar an gclaí
Is dearc ar an ainmhí is duine,
Dearc ar an bhfiach
Is ar chath na colla,
Is meabhraigh an gníomh
Nach bhfuil ina leath ach tuirse.
A dúirt an croí:
Is corrach do shuí
Go héag na hola.

DIALOGUE

Said reason:
Live regardless
Of the raised breasts,
The armoury of guile,
The secrets of courtship,
The slender body,
The flowing tresses.
Said heart:
Where is my tithe
Till the hour of extreme unction?

Said reason:
Sit on the fence
And look at man the animal,
Look at the strivings
And struggles of flesh,
And think of the act
That is half remorse.
Said heart:
You will not stand easy
Till the hour of extreme unction.

DOM FÉIN

Tar ar do chéill feasta
Tá an leathchéad go tréan
Ar na sála agat,
Níl ribe ar do bhlaosc
Ná meigeall ar do smig
Is bean aosta féin
Ní ghlacfadh dán uait.

TO MYSELF

Come to your senses now
Your fifty years are close
On your heels,
You haven't a hair on your head
Or a beard on your chin;
Even a crone
Would reject your poem.

DÉITHE BRÉIGE

Maise a sheanpháiste
A chuir déithe in airde,
Ná tóg ar na déithe
Má léimeadar anuas
Faoi do chosa,
Is má chaith gach dia
A choróin leat aniar
Is an fhonóid ina diaidh
Sna sála ort.

FALSE GODS

Well then, you dotard
Who set up gods,
Don't blame the gods
If they leaped down
Right at your feet,
And each god hurled
His crown at your back,
Derisive laughter following
Hard on your heels.

REILIG

Cuireadh an ghealach
Aisléine bhán ar gach leacht,
Gach crois gach gloine fhuar
A chumhdaíonn blátha ar uaigh
I ngarraí gabhainn na marbh.

Déanadh sibhse faire claí
Is seasaíg garda a fhallaí arda,
Is ná tagadh siosma baoise
Ó shlí na bréige,
An fhaid atá cnámha bána
Ag comhrá le cnámh gealaí.

CEMETERY

Let the moon lay
A white shroud on each headstone,
Each cross, each chill glass
That enshrines flowers on a grave
In the locked garden of the dead.

Keep the dead man's watch
And stand on guard, you high walls,
And let no idle whisper come
From life's deceitful way
While white bones
Converse with a bone moon.

AN SMIOTA

An bhlaosc chrón chríon sa scrín
San eaglais cois na Bóinne
Níor bhain an smiota de do bhéal,
Ach b'áil liom a fhiafraí
Céard a thug tú chun na háite
Ó mheasas nárbh údar blaosc chun gáire,
Is cheapas gur rugadh tú in antráth
Is dá mairteá le linn Herod Rí,
Go dtabharfá blaosc an Naoimh isteach
Is aoibh an gháire ort.

THE SMIRK

That yellow, dried-up skull in the shrine
In the church beside the Boyne
Didn't wipe that smirk from your mouth,
But I wanted to ask
What brought you there
Since I judged a skull no cause for laughter,
And I thought to myself you'd been born too late
For if you'd lived when Herod was king,
You would have brought the Saint's head in
With a smile on your lips.

NA COILLTEÁIN

'Cuirimis le chéile' a deir na coillteáin
Ionas nach léifear faisnéis
Ar ghinte an fhir seo
Ar pháipéar ná in irisleabhar:
Is chuireadar le chéile
Ag ól na dí dóibh
I gcúinní an fhill,
Óir níl éad níos géire
Ná éad an choillteáin
Le fear na gcloch.

THE EUNUCHS

'Let's collaborate' say the eunuchs
So no account will be read
Of what this man fathered,
Not in paper nor journal:
And they collaborated,
Downing their drinks
In the evil alcoves,
For there's no keener envy
Than that of the eunuch
For the man with balls.

CEANNAITHE

Ceist a chuirtí tráth
Más fíor na ráite
'Cén áit in nGaillimh
A bhfuil Éire ann?'
Gach prionsa ceannaí
Dár thabhaigh cáil di,
Tá gan oidhre
Ar a áit,
Is b'aithnid dúinne
Toicithe glacacha,
Nach gcloisfear
A dtrácht sa Spáinn.

MERCHANTS

It used to be asked,
If it's true what they say,
'Where in Galway
Can Ireland be found?'
Each merchant prince
Who won her that fame
Has left no heir
To fill his place
And we have known
Grasping tycoons
Whose names won't be heard
Mentioned in Spain.

AN DUAIS

Prealáid ina dhún féin,
Manach ina chillín fuarghlas,
Máthairab ina suanlios,
Mise i lios an léinn aréir
Mar a dtagann dán le dua liom;
Íocaimid go léir deachú an uaignis.

Gheobhaidh an triúr an duais fós
Is luach a saothair sa tír uachtraigh,
Ach faighim féin an duais gach lá,
Is luach mo shaothair go dóite:
Gáire an dúiste i mo dhiaidh aniar,
Uaill an choillteáin i mo chluasa,
Is an t-uaigneas suas liom cuachta.

THE REWARD

A prelate in his own palace,
A monk in his cold grey cell,
An abbess in her dormitory,
And I in learning's garth* last night
Where my poems have troubled birth —
We all pay the solitary's tithe.

Those three will get their reward
And their labour's wage in the land above,
But I receive my reward each day,
My labour's wage in bitter bile:
Loutish laughter behind me,
The eunuch's howl in my ears
And loneliness curled up close to me.

*courtyard, garden . . . [Publisher's note]

91

BUÍOCHAS

Mithid dom mo bhuíochas
A ghabháil libh a dhúile,
An comhar a dhíol libh
A chreaga loma,
A fharraigí cháite,
A chuireadh deocha
Go lách faoi mo ghruanna,
Nuair nach mbíodh cara cáis agam
A d'fhulaingeodh m'ualach,
Ná a d'osclódh doras an fheasa
Sa dún diamhair do mo fhuascailt,
Is neart na tola dorcha
Ag borradh chugamsa.

GRATITUDE

It's time I made my gratitude
Known to you, you elements,
That I repaid your help,
You bare crags,
You foaming seas
That used to lave
My cheeks so gently
When I had none to confide in,
None who would bear my burden
And open wisdom's door
Inside the enchanted castle to save me
When the force of the dark will
Surged towards me.

FUAIRE

Luí ar mo chranna foirtil!
Céard eile a dhéanfainn féin
Ó tá mála an tsnáith ghil
Folamh i do pháirt go héag?
Ach tá a fhios ag mo chroí,
Cé goirt le roinnt an scéal,
Go bhfuil na cranna céanna
Chomh fuar leis an spéir.

COLDNESS

Lean on my stout oars!
What else could I have done
Since the purse where I kept the bright thread
Is empty of your love for ever?
But my heart knows,
Though confessing it is bitter,
That those selfsame oars
Are as cold as the sky.

ÉIRE INA bhFUIL ROMHAINN

An té a nocht a chlaíomh go hard
I do pháirt um Cháisc na lasrach,
Má shíl gur shaor tú ón iomad náire
Nach cuma, óir ní raibh ann ach fear saonta
Is file laochta nár cruinníodh leis stór,
Is nár fhág ina dhiaidh ach glóir;
Cuirfear iallach ort a ghlóir a dhíol,
Faoi mar ab éigean duit roimh a theacht
A bheith i do thráill ag gach bodach anall,
Is má thugtar meas méirdrí arís ort
Bí i do mhéirdrigh mhóir dáiríre,
Is díol a ghlóir is tabhair a sháith
Do gach bodach aniar chun éilimh,
Reic fós a mhian is beir i do threo
Céile nua is a stór chun leapan,
Mar ní tú feasta céile Choinn ná Eoghain,
Céile an Phiarsaigh ná rún na laoch,
Ach más éigean an cumann a chur i gcrích
Agraim thú a shearc na bhFiann,
Gan ceangal leo gan raidhse dollar.

TO IRELAND IN THE COMING TIMES

The man who bared his blade on high
In your defence when Easter blazed —
If he thought he'd freed you from too much shame,
What odds! He was only a simple fellow,
A poet-hero who had nothing saved
And nothing to bequeath but glory;
His glory you'll be forced to sell,
As you were compelled, before he came,
To be the slave of each foreign lout,
And if you're looked on as a whore again
Play the famous whore in earnest
And sell his glory and satiate
Each lout who sidles up to solicit,
Betray his ideal as well and lead
A new mate and his wealth to bed,
For you're no longer the mate of Conn nor Eoghan,
The mate of Pearse nor the beloved of heroes,
But if the attachment must be consummated
Let me beseech you, you darling of the Fianna,
To make no contract without wads of dollars.

MAR CHAITHEAMAR AN CHOINNEAL

Cheapamar tráth go mbeadh an lá linn
An bua ar fáil, an t-athaoibhneas ag teacht,
Is chaitheamar an choinneal de ráig
Ag fónamh dár gcleacht;
Ní náir linn os comhair cáich
Ár gcloichín ar charn na sean,
Cé gur eagal linn le seal
Go bhfuilimid ag cur gainimh i ngad,
Murar i gCionn tSáile an léin
A cuireadh ár gcleacht ó rath,
Arbh iad na cinnirí críonna
Nó cléirigh an tréis a d'fheall?
Ach mar chuaigh an choinneal go dtí seo,
Téadh an t-orlach ina bhfuil romhainn amach.

HOW WE WASTED THE CANDLE

Once we thought the day would be ours,
The victory gained, the old joy returning,
And we burned the candle prodigally
In the service of our cause.
We are not ashamed before any one
Of our pebble on the ancestral cairn,
Though I fear that of late
Our rope binds only sand;
If it was not in Kinsale of the sorrow
That our civilisation was ruined,
Was it the cautious leaders
Or the treacherous clerks that reneged?
But as the candle has wasted till now
Let the last inch waste in the time to come.

RÉIM NA bhFAOILEÁN

Na seabhaic thréana
Ní léir go bhfillfidh,
Is follas nach é
A lá atá ann:
An ladhrán trá
Ná an chorr éisc
An fada eile a mhairfidh
Ar chladaí fiara?
Pór na heala
Is an t-éan fionn,
Imeoidh fós ina ndiaidh,
Ach an faoileán amplach
Gona gharbhghlór gránna
Fanfaidh i bhfeighil a choda
In aice an chonúis bhréin:
A mhalairt níor chleacht an t-éan.

THE RULE OF THE GULLS

The great hawks
May not return;
It's clear that this
Is not their day:
Will the redshank
Or the long-legged heron
Survive much longer
On stormy strands?
The swan's brood
And the white sea-eagle
Will follow them away,
But the voracious gull
With its grating squawk
Will jealously guard its share
Of repulsive carrion —
That bird's accustomed fare.

GNÍOMH GOIMHE

Toirtín goirt a thriall chugam
Mo litir orm a chas tú:
Gníomh goimhe, is buille
Ó do láimhse thug amas.

Goirt óna fhilleadh orm
Gan mé á aisghairm,
An snáth trínar mheasas
Gad caidrimh a athshníomh.

Tréith mé fós ón tuairt
A bhuail mé ar maidin,
A chuaigh go dtí an dóbair
Do m'arann é a ghlasadh.

Cén chúis agat orm
Fá rachfá chun ainchinn?
Cion ar bith a luafá liom
Ceann corrach faoi deara é?

Sin agus gach ala
D'fhuíoll an ghnáthaimh,
Bheith in áirithe don bhé bhán
Ag a bhfuil m'anam.

Ar riar na gcúram bheadh breith
Ag mo leithéid féin mheasas,
Ach gnó an dáin ní fhulaingeann
Drogall uaim ná neamart.   ▶

A SPITEFUL DEED

It was a bitter recompense
When you sent back my letter:
A spiteful deed, and a blow
Thrust home from your hand.

Bitter because it came back to me,
Without my retracting it,
The thread with which I thought
To respin the rope of intimacy.

I am still weak from the shock
Which struck me this morning,
Which almost succeeded
In numbing my senses.

What do you hold against me
That would cause you to sulk?
That any fault you might mention
Was caused by an unsteady mind?

That, and because each moment
Left over from the daily round
Is reserved for the bright muse
Who has my soul.

There'd be time for chores to be done
By the likes of me, I thought,
But the poetic task doesn't tolerate
Disinclination or neglect.

▶

File mé is ní fealsamh,
Ach ó scarais le do stuaim
Is fearr liom san uaimh dhubh
Ná dul leat faoin bhfearthainn.

Dá bhfágtaí Lá an Luain
An bhreith ar do láimh
Peacach ní bhfaigheadh logha
Ná maitheamh uait go brách.

I'm a poet, not a philosopher,
But since you've lost your composure
I'd rather stay in the dark cave
Than walk with you in the rain.

If on the day of Judgement
The decision were left in your hand,
No sinner would get remission
Or forgiveness from you for ever.

BERKELEY

Ar charraig, a Easpaig Chluana,
A tógadh mise i mo ghasúr
Is bhí na clocha glasa
Is na creaga loma fúm is tharam,
Ach b'fhada uathu a mhair tusa
A Easpaig is a fhealsaimh.

Swift féin an Déan mór
Níorbh ait fós má b'fhíor
Gur fhág tú ar a thairsigh;
Comhla an dorais nár bhrionglóid
I do mheabhair de réir do theagaisc?
Is cad ab áil leis a hoscailt duit
Is gan ann ach a samhail?

An Dochtúir Johnson fós
Thug speach do chloch ina aice
Mar dhóigh go ndearna an buille
Ar an rud ionraic smionagar
De do aisling, a chuir i gcás
Gur istigh san aigne a bhí
Gach ní beo is marbh.

Ní shéanaim go raibh mo pháirt
Leis na móir úd tamall,
Ach ó thosaigh na clocha glasa
Ag dul i gcruth brionglóide i m'aigne
Níl a fhios agam a Easpaig chóir
Nach tú féin a chuaigh ar an domhain
Is nach iad na móir a d'fhan le cladach.

BERKELEY

On a rock, Bishop of Cloyne,
I was reared as a boy;
And the grey stones
And barren crags encompassed me,
But far from such you lived,
Bishop and philosopher.

Swift himself, the great Dean,
Was not mad, if it's true
He left you on his doorstep;
Was not the closed door a dream
In your mind, for thus you taught?
And why would he want to open it for you
Since it was only a ghost of itself?

Dr. Johnson too
Kicked an adjacent stone
As if the assault
On the pure entity smashed
Your vision, and its implication
That in the mind was contained
All living substance and all inanimate matter.

I don't deny I agreed
With those great men for a while,
But since the grey stones began
To turn to dreams in my mind,
I do not know, my dear Bishop,
That you weren't the one who went on the deep
While the great men stayed on the shore.

CLANN CHÁIN

Líonmhar iad clann Cháin
A mharc orthu is léir;
Clann Abel d'fhiach
A mian is a ndearbhdháil.

Ní leor dlí na treibhe,
In ollchathair níl feidhm aici,
Ní coimeádaí a bhráthar aon fhear;
A ngaol atá i bhfad amach.

Ní mó is leor dlí Dé
Don dream nach ní leo é;
Dia nua is rogha leo,
Forneart a ainm is éigean.

Ar an talamh tá fós béal
A d'ólfadh fuil as láimh,
Fuil a dhéanfadh éamh
Is scéal ar an mharfóir.

Cosán crua coincréite
Ní ólann fuil as láimh;
Níl béal air don ghnó
Is ní dhéanann scéal ar an mharfóir.

THE CHILDREN OF CAIN

The children of Cain have multiplied,
They flaunt his mark;
Hunting down the children of Abel
Is their desire and their final cause.

The law of the tribe is inadequate,
It serves no function in megalopolis,
No one is his brother's keeper;
Their kinship is too far removed.

God's law itself is inadequate
For those who deny it exists;
They've chosen a new god
Named violence and rapine.

The earth has still a mouth
To drink blood from a hand,
Blood that would cry out
And name the murderer.

Hard concrete pavements
Do not drink blood from a hand;
They have no mouth to open,
They leave the murderer unnamed.

UALACH

Ní ualach go hualach uabhair,
Ní uabhar go huabhar file
A fhásann as móiréis na dáimhe:
An fhaid atá tógáil a phinn ina láimh
Tá tógáil a chinn ann,
Is bráithre ina dháil
Ag sníomh le briathra.

Ní umhlaíocht a umhlaíocht
Ach folach priacail;
Is freastal an dá thrá
A chuireann a mheabhair ar fán,
Is a fhágann ina lár
Geit nach den aiteas riamh di.

Ní chuirfí poll ar a onóir
Dá mairfeadh cion ar an mbriathar,
Ach ó chuaigh an briathar ó chion
Is minic ise ina criathar.

Cabhair dá ngoirfeadh Aogán
Níor ghairide dó an ní;
Geallaim nár ghairide fós
Dá ndéanfadh inniu a ghuí.

BURDEN

There is no burden like the burden of pride,
There is no pride like the pride of a poet
Which springs from his exalted calling:
While he can lift his pen in his hand
He can lift his head
And join his peers
In the weaving of words.

His humility is not humility
But danger's disguise;
And coping with the two strands
Sets his mind astray
And leaves in his heart
A tension that never springs from delight.

There would be no chink in his honour
If words were still regarded with love,
But since the love of words has gone
His honour has often been turned into a sieve.

If Aogan had called for succour
It would have come no nearer his way;
I warrant it would still be no nearer
If he made his plea today.

GLÓR ACASTÓRA

Cá bhfuilir uaim le fada
A ghlór acastóra?
Thiar i gcúl an ama atáir
Cé gur iomaí oíche i bhfad ó shin
Ba cheol tú i mo chluasa.

Carr Aindí Goill ar chapall maith
Bhíodh ag dul in aghaidh aird
Ar a bhealach go hEoghanacht.
Deireann súile m'aigne liom
Go raibh péint ghlé dhearg air,
Ach ní hé sin is measa liom
Ná is mó a airím uaim,
Ach glór an acastóra
A bhogadh chun suain mé.

AXLE SONG

Where have you been this long time,
Song of the axle?
Hidden in time's backyard
Though many a night long ago
You were music to my ears.

Andy Goill's cart behind a good horse
Was climbing the slope
On the way to Ownaght.
My mind's eye tells me
It was painted bright red,
But that's not my keenest memory
Nor what I miss the most,
But the song of the axle
That lulled me to sleep.

CUING GHNÁIS

An fear a chaith splanc ón tine chnámh
Isteach i ngarraí an dorais
Níorbh eol dó athair an ghnímh a rinne;
Ach chomhlíon cuing ghnáis,
A rinne aon chine amháin
De chlann an fhóid anall
Ón Ind go dtí An Sruthán.

THE YOKE OF CUSTOM

The man who cast an ember from the bonfire
Into the garden outside his door
Didn't know the father of his deed;
But he fulfilled the dictate of a custom
That made one clan
Of all the tillers of the soil
From India to Sruthán.

BILE A THIT

(Ómós do Mháirtín Ó Cadhain)

Fuil na bua a théachtaigh
Is bile ár gcleacht a thit:
Tásc na tubaiste fuaire
A rinne oighear den mheidhir sna fir.

Ba feannta an uair í,
Ba chaillte an mhaidin,
Ar leagadh san uaigh tú,
Is cé nach í cré do mhuintire
A dáileadh síos leat
Ní miste an cumasc duitse
A ghlac chugat Éire uile
Le páirt is tairise di.

Mallmhuir ní luaifear leat
Ná go brách lagtrá:
Ba rabharta a théadh thar maoil
Do bhruth is do chumas;
Ach is olc a théann an rabharta
Ar an mallmhuir dúinne.

Le fíoch ba mhinic a d'fhiuchais,
Truabhail do chleacht
A líon do racht gur scaoil.

Mura ndeachaigh namhaid ná cara féin slán
Ó aghaidh do chraois
Maitear a lán do rí an fhocail;
Maithfear duitse mar sin —
I do rí gan freasúra a chuais go Cill. ▶

THE TREE THAT FELL

(Homage to Máirtín Ó Cadhain)

Clotted our triumphant blood!
Fallen tradition's sacred tree!
The cold obit of disaster
Has turned men's joy to ice.

It was bitter weather,
It was a bleak morning
That they laid you in the grave,
And though it was not your own kin's clay
They scattered over you
Such mingling leaves you undisturbed —
You who embraced the whole of Ireland
In loyalty and in love.

Neap-tide will not be ascribed to you
Nor ever the withdrawing ebb:
A springtide's flood
Your seething force;
But the springtide ill accords
With our neap-tide.

You often boiled with fury,
Your tradition's dereliction
Swelled your heart to bursting.

If neither friend nor enemy escaped
Your abrasive tongue,
Much is forgiven the king of the word:
Much will be forgiven you —
King without opposition you entered the burial ground.

▶

Ach ní tú thit ann:
Meirge Mhurchú a thit arís,
Cionn tSáile eile a briseadh orainn,
Eachroim an Áir is Scairbhsholais.

But it was not you who fell:
Murchu's banner fell once more,
We suffered defeat at another Kinsale,
Another Aughrim and Scarifhollis.

NEAMHIONRAIC GACH BEO

Nuair a bhí tine is ól mar dhíon
Ar shíon na hoíche fuaire
Ba bhurla beag beadaí tú
I dteas na tine os do chomhair
Is ó mheidhir an fhíona taobh leat;
Ach d'aird fós ar do ghnó
In ainneoin tine, óil is teasa,
Ach ní rabhais ionraic ar oileán
Ná aon duine den bhuín a bhí i do theannta.

An seantriath ar an mballa
Gona mhéadal nósmhar,
Is a chaofach mná thall
Gona brollach nósmhar,
Atá ceaptha in dhá phortráid
Atá neamhbheo gan malairt
Le trí chéad bliain is breis —
Táid beirt ionraic ar oileán,
Mar tá cloch carraig is trá
I lár na hoíche fuaire.

Sleamhnaíonn nithe neamhbheo
Siar ón mbeo go bhfágann é:
An amhlaidh sin a d'fhág
An t-oileán mo dhán,
Nó ar thugais faoi deara é?

THE ESSENCE IS NOT IN THE LIVING

When fire and drink were a shelter
From the blast of the cold night
You were a compact bundle of sensuousness —
The warmth of the fire before you,
The cheering wine at your side;
But you were still intent on your interests
In spite of fire, drink and warmth,
But you were not the essence of an island
Nor any of the group who were with you.

The old lord on the wall
With his formal paunch,
And his good lady facing him
With her formal bust,
Have been captured in two portraits
Unliving and unchanged
For three hundred years and more —
Those two are the essence of an island,
As are stone rock and strand
In the cold midnight.

Unliving things slip
Away from life and leave it:
Was it thus
The island left my poem,
Or did you notice?

COGAR NA NATHRACH

Dá dtéadh gach bean in éag ach tú
Ionas go mba tusa féin a gcrot go léir,
Peaca Ádhaimh níorbh ait le héinne beo,
Is chuirfí glasa daingne ar gach úllghort lán
Ar eagla slad ar úll na haithne.

Chím i dtnúth do ghnúise rite,
Is i do leabharchorp cuartha cailce,
Dúshlán gach cime a thug móid na cuinge,
Gan taise i d'fhéachaint ach tarcaisne dósan,
Ní saoirse ach daoirse don chime gabháil leat.

Beirir as suan chun cuimhne fir
Uille ar ghlúin is sioscadh cois tine,
Gáire coimeádach i gcoim oíche as cúinne,
Leidí beaga fáin ar rún gach mná agaibh
A fuair máthair an chine ón nathair i gcogar fill.

THE SERPENT'S WHISPER

If every woman died but you
And you yourself embodied them all,
Not a soul would wonder at Adam's sin;
Stout locks would be placed on each full orchard
Lest the Apple of Knowledge be stolen.

I see in your face that is tense with longing,
In the curving grace of your limewhite body,
A challenge to each slave sworn to the yoke;
Your pitiless glance shows you despise him;
Who goes with you is thrall, not free.

You lift a man's mind to his sleeping memory
Of elbow on knee and fireside whisper,
The knowing chuckle from a night-dark corner:
Small random hints of all women's secret
Obtained by Eve from the serpent in a treacherous
    whisper.

AN AGHAIDH SIN ORT

Tabhair aire don aghaidh sin!
Ní leat í go huile,
Ach í agat ar iasacht
Ó mhná daingne ár gcine.

Nuair a sínim mo chuimhne
Ar chéad bean a chím í,
Mná ár gcine ó cuireadh
Thar Ghaillimh siar iad.

Mná a d'fhoghlaim foighid
Ó fhanacht fhada righin
Ar thoradh silte
D'fhág a séala uirthi.

Séala eile ar an aghaidh sin
Ó mhná a cheileadh an bród
Tráth a bhfaighidís an déirc
Ba pholl ar a n-onóir.

Clann na Gaeilge atá roinnte
Ar chlár na cruinne,
Gan stát acu ná rialtas
Gan ceann ina bhfochair.

Tabhair aire don aghaidh sin,
Ní leat í go huile,
Ach í agat ar iasacht
Ó mhná daingne ár gcine.

THAT FACE

Take care of that face!
It is not fully yours
But you have it on loan
From the staunch women of our race.

When I stretch my memory
I see it on a hundred women —
The women of our people who were sent
Beyond Galway to the West.

Women who learned forbearance
During the long slow wait
For the pitiable reward —
They left their mark on that face.

There is another mark on that face —
Of women who hid their pride
The time they got the alms
That left a chink in their honour.

The speakers of Irish are scattered
Around the surface of the globe
Without government or state,
Without a leader among them.

Take care of that face!
It is not fully yours
But you have it on loan
From the staunch women of our race.

NOTES

Ó Mórna

The first verse refers to the graveyard above the strand to the south of Kilmurvey in Aran.

There is an inscription in the graveyard which reads as follows:

Pray for the repose
of the soul of
Patrick O Flaherty J.P.
the fond father of
James O Flaherty
who departed this life
A.D. 1864 aged 82 years
R.I.P.
Sacred to the memory of
James O Flaherty J.P.
Kilmurvey House who departed
this life Oc^r 24th A.D. 1881
aged 64 years
Fortified by the last rites
of Holy Church
R.I.P.
Blessed are the dead who die in the Lord

Verse 5. The *umar bréige* or makeshift trough was usually a door taken off its hinges, on which the newly-woven cloth, soaked in urine, would be laid and round which the women would sit, pounding the cloth with their feet in order to shrink and thicken it.

Ó Mórna's isolation and the failure of his marriage are made more explicit in the first version of the poem (which is reproduced in full in *Dánta 1939-1979*):

Ó Briain, Mac Conmara
Ó Domhnalláin ná Ó Ceallaigh
Níor mhinic a dtriall
Ar an triath le báidh,
Ó Máille ní thagadh
Ná a bhean ina theannta,
Is Blácaigh níorbh áil
I ndáil leis feasta,
Is bhíodh leathmhaing dhona
Ar a shaol de ghnáth.

Bhí céile leapa aige le haimsir

127

Ach níor luigh léi anois aon oíche le fada,
Meas deoir aille thug uirthi ar fhuaire,
Is ina cuilt shuain ní bhfuair aon taithneamh:
Ó Mórna pósta is céasta in éineacht.

Clann iníon do rug dó
Is ní oighre dílis fir,
Ceann fine gan fine
Gan oighre ceart ar a dháil,
Minic dúirt trína mheisce
Gur mhairg a shínfeadh
Le Blácach mná . . .

(O'Brien, Macnamara
O'Donnellan and O'Kelly
Seldom visited
The chief in friendship,
O'Malley didn't come
Nor his wife along with him,
And the Blakes didn't care
For his company any longer,
Badly off balance
Was his life always.

He'd had a wife for some time
But hadn't slept with her now for ages,
He thought her as cold as the seepage from a cliff,
And he got no pleasure in her drowsy bed:
Ó Mórna married and at the same time tormented.

She bore him daughters
Instead of a lawful male heir;
A tribeless head of a tribe
With no proper heir in his place,
He often said in his cups
That only a fool would lie
With a woman Blake . . .)

The O'Briens had been lords of Aran in mediaeval times, the
Macnamaras were a prominent family in Co. Clare, the O'Donnellans
and the O'Kellys, both descended from the same stock, were powerful
families in Co. Galway, and O'Malley was the tenant of the Hill Farm
near Killeany, Aran, in the 1830s — it would appear that Ó Mórna
was almost ostracised by the members of his own class.
    The line 'Ó Mórna married and at the same time tormented' recalls
the Irish proverb *Ní céasta go pósta* (There's no torment like
marriage).

Deireadh Ré *(End of an Era)*
Oisín was a member of the Fianna, a warrior band of the fifth century. According to the legend he left Ireland to live with his fairy bride and when he returned he was aghast to find no trace of his companions. He narrated their history to St Patrick before he died. *Oisín i ndiaidh na Féinne* (Oisín after the Fianna) has become a proverbial expression.

Ómós do John Millington Synge *(Homage to John Millington Synge)*
J. M. Synge made lengthy visits to the Aran Islands in 1898, 1899, 1900 and 1901. On his first visit he spent a fortnight on Inishmore and visited all the ruins, monuments and holy places, but he spent the remaining four weeks on Inishmaan, staying in the post-office, to which he was to return on subsequent visits. He spent much of his time listening to the celebrated story-teller Páraic Ó Direáin (Pat Dirrane). Nearly all his plays owe something to his visits to the Aran Islands. He began translating the old story of Deirdre and Naoise there in 1901 and the plot of 'The Playboy of the Western World' was suggested by a story heard on Inishmaan. Ceann Gainimh (Sandy Headland) is at the north eastern corner of Inishmaan. Coill Chuain (The Wood of Cuan) is one of the places in the West of Scotland where Deirdre and Naoise lived during their exile.

Teampall an Cheathrair Álainn *(The Church of the Four Beautiful Ones)*
A ruined fifteenth-century church near Corrúch in Inishmore. There are four horizontal tombstones side by side in the enclosure outside the eastern gable of the church. None of the stones bears any inscription.

Teaghlach Éanna *(Éanna's Community)*
St Éanna or Enda was born in the middle of the fifth century and became Chief of Oriel (a district coextensive with the present diocese of Clogher, comprising Counties Fermanagh and Monaghan) on the death of his father. He resigned the title and established a monastery near Killeany on Inishmore about the year 480. The fame of Aran as a holy place, *Ára na Naomh* (Aran of the Saints), spread to Europe and for some hundreds of years people came to its monasteries. Éanna's monastery was the principal monastery of Aran. He is said to be buried along with 120 of his followers in the graveyard, now covered with sand, to the north of the ruined church called Teaghlach Éinne, parts of which may date back to the eighth century. Sand threatens to encroach on the church.

129

An Stailc *(The Strike)*

The strike referred to occurred in Galway during Ó Direáin's sojourn in that city. This is one of a number of poems which indicate the poet's sense of solidarity with the working class, which is given its most forceful expression in an early uncollected poem — *Séamus Ó Conghaile* (James Connolly):

Le bánú a' lae i mbliadhain a sé-déag,
Tnáithe, faon-lag, cráidhte ag créachtaibh,
Ceangailte go dlúth de chathaoir na bpian duit
'Seadh teilgeadh t'anam i láthair Mhic Dé uait.

Dá n-abruigheadh neach leat maidin a' lae úd
Go mbeadh daoine an tráth seo ar fud do thíre
Bheadh bocht is nocht, gan a gcoinne le aon rud
Acht an-shógh is cáll, is iad beó ar dhéirce

Déarfá féin leis gurbh éitheach a fhís duit
Go mbeadh fuigheall gach fuighill 'rís ag Gaedhealaibh
'S sógh is sonas i ndán do gach aon díobh,
De thoradh t'íodhbairt' is íodhbairt' gach laoich dhíbh.

Acht is truagh le n-aithris an scéal 'tá amhlaidh,
Fiche bliadhain is cúig ó thuit tú go calma;
Fir mhóra láidre is a ndruim le balla
'S ocras is fuacht ar bhean is ar leanbh.

Lucht maoin is rachmais suidhte go daingean;
Iad súighte, báidhte, i bpléisiúir shaoghalta;
Iad seascair, caomhnuighthe i dtighthibh teólaidh;
A gcoinsias maolaithe is gan carthannacht a' gabháil leo.

Leanbhaí óga ar gheall Dia saoghal dóibh,
Ar gheall Sé oighreacht, sonas is séan dóibh
In áithridhe* ag eitinn roimh theacht i méid dóibh
Toisc bheith plóduighthe plúchta i seómraibh caol' cumhang'.

Fir luath' láidre a' fágáil na tíre
'S mná breágth' mánla ar siubhal mar aon leo
'S dian-ghádh deacrach leo in Éirinn
'Tá íseal cheana i líon a daoine.

Acht caithfidh Gaedhil feasta choidhche
An córas malluighthe a bhriseadh is a réabadh,
A chreach ó thús 's a chuir in ísle-bhrí sinn
'S córas nua a chur in uachtar i nÉirinn.

*áirithe

130

Ar theacht an lae sin a fhir mhóir a' mhisnigh,
Bhéarfar onóir chóir dhuit is díbh go h-uile,
A thuit gan staonadh is fós gan cliseadh,
Le bánú a' lae ghil annseo cois Life.

(On a bright day's dawning in the year sixteen
Wearied and weakened by loss of blood,
You were tightly bound to your chair of pain
And your soul was blasted to the presence of Jesus.

If someone had said to you on that morning
That there would be people now throughout your land
Poor and naked, expecting nothing
But misery and want and living by beggary

You'd have told him yourself his vision was calumny,
That every Gael would have enough and to spare,
That joy and content were in store for each one of them
Won by the blood offered by you and your comrades.

But sad to relate that's the way it turned out
Twenty-five years since you bravely fell;
Big sturdy men with their backs to the wall,
And women and children hungry and cold.

The rich and the wealthy are firmly established;
Steeped and drowned in worldly pleasure;
Snug and sheltered in well-warmed houses;
Their conscience numbed and charity unknown to them.

Young children whom God promised life to,
Promised a birthright, joy and prosperity,
Are secured for T.B. before they grow up
By being packed to suffocation in cramped narrow rooms.

Fine strong men are leaving the country
And fine handsome women are going along with them
Though they are desperately needed here in an Ireland
Whose population is already diminished.

From now on the Gael must always
Smash and shatter the accursed system
That first plundered and then left us weakened
And bring a new order to triumph in Ireland.

When that day comes, great-hearted comrade,
You'll be rightly honoured and all you others
Who fell unyielding and died unflinching
On a bright day's dawning by the Liffeyside.)

131

Na Turais *(The Pilgrimages)*
'During my youth the pilgrimages were of great importance. People came over from Conamara and lived among us for a week perhaps, when the holy days occurred . . . Then when the vigil came, the vigil of St John's Day, or any other vigil of the kind, they used to go to the Seven Churches, the nearest place of pilgrimage, and sleep there till morning, along with some of our neighbours. There were no priests or monks with them, but they used to recite all of the rosary and make the round of a holy well.'

Cranna Foirtil *(Stout Oars)*
The poem is held together by its play on some of the many meanings of the word *crann*; tree, timber, piece of wood, staff, shaft, oar, stick and so on — a *crann* can be almost any thing made of wood from a bedstead to a harp. The *cranna foirtil* of the title are firm supports; the *cranna cosanta* stood for a palisade of domestic items that used to be placed by a baby's cradle to defend him from the good people, evil spirits etc.; the *cranna caillte* are the withered or dead twigs which along with the other articles mentioned helped to avert evil, though the use of the word *caillte* strongly suggests that the twigs were not only dead but useless: the poet has only his own *cranna foirtil*, his trees, his staves, his props, his oars, to save him from retreating with the ebb to a perpetual low water.

Olc Liom *(Remorse)*
Dónall an tSrutháin: Great-great-grandfather of Máirtín Ó Direáin.

Sic Transit . . .
Clann Mhic Thaidhg: a sept of the O'Briens of North Munster are said to have been overlords of the Aran Islands from the eleventh to the sixteenth centuries.

Verse 2. Na flatha a bhris a réim (The lords who broke their sway) were the O'Flaherties of Connaught. In the nineteenth century they were still the principal tenant-farmers, the islands belonging to absentee landlords called Digby. Patrick O'Flaherty, J.P. (1782-1864), lived like a king in Kilmurvey House. His son, James O'Flaherty, was execrated as a landgrabber in the 1880s.

Verse 3. Compare with the first verse of *Ó Mórna*.

Trá na gCeann (The Strand of the Heads)
According to tradition an internecine battle took place here among the O'Briens and skulls have been dug up at the site.

132

De Dheasca an Úis *(Because of Usury)*
Dr Ó Direáin has told us that he was greatly influenced by Ezra Pound's economic theories and the title of this poem echoes Pound's 'With Usura'.

Cuid Caidéise *(Curiosity)*
Fód teallaigh (Mensal lands): lands set aside for the maintenance of the table.

Coill Chuain
See note on *Ómós do John Millington Synge*.

Reilig *(Cemetery)*
This is the graveyard in Templeogue just outside Dublin. The poet often walked past it at night.

faire claí (dead man's watch): 'when a body was buried in a graveyard, the people thought it would have to keep watch on the boundary till the next body came'.

An Smiota *(The Smirk)*
The embalmed head of Blessed Oliver Plunkett (1621-81), Archbishop of Armagh, who was hanged, drawn and quartered at Tyburn, is enshrined in St Peter's Church, Drogheda.

Ceannaithe *(Merchants)*
By the sixteenth century Galway had become one of the greatest ports in these islands, and from the fair of Santiago de Compostela in N.E. Spain, which was the centre of the Galway trade, Irish merchants spread over Spain and Portugal. The question in the poem is taken from Peter Heylin (1600-1662), a voluminous writer mostly on ecclesiastical subjects, and is quoted in *Oileáin Árainn* (1930) by an tAthair Mártán Ó Domhnaill.

Fuaire *(Coldness)*
mála an tsnáith ghil (purse . . . of bright thread): 'the women who did knitting long ago used to put the bright thread, the best thread, aside in a little bag; they used to make special clothes for somebody they would be fond of. Here it is a symbol of the loved one — one you would keep in the purse of bright thread.'

Éire ina bhfuil Romhainn *(To Ireland in the Coming Times)*
Conn: Conn of the Hundred Battles, king of Ireland in the second century.

133

Eoghan: Owen Roe O'Neill, who defeated a Scottish army under Munro at the Battle of Benburb in Co. Tyrone, 1646.

Mar Chaitheamar an Choinneal *(How We Wasted the Candle)*
Kinsale: The defeat of the Irish at the Battle of Kinsale in 1602 led to the Flight of the Earls and the disappearance of the old Gaelic order.

Gníomh Goimhe *(A Spiteful Deed)*
Verse 7 refers to an apologue in a poem by Eochaidh Ó hEodhusa, written about 1590. Thirty philosophers warned the people that a shower was coming that would deprive them of their wits. The philosophers sheltered in a cave but when they emerged found that the people could no longer understand them. They decided they might as well go out in the rain and be as foolish as everyone else. 'To go out in the rain' became a proverbial expression.

Ualach *(Burden)*
Aogán Ó Rathaille (c.1665-c.1728) in a poem composed on his deathbed, said:

Cabhair ní ghairfead go gcuirthear mé i gcruinnchomhrainn —
Dar an leabhar dá ngairinn níor ghairide an ní dhomhsa . . .

(I will not call for succour until I am placed in a narrow coffin — By the book, if I were to call, it would come no nearer . . .)

freastal an dá thrá (cope with the two strands) is a reference to the proverb: *Ní thig leis an ngobadán an dá thrá do fhreastal* (The rock-pipit cannot attend to the two strands or two ebb tides), i.e. one cannot do two things at once or cannot work all day.

Glór Acastóra *(Axle Song)*
Eoghanacht (Ownaght): the next village to the west of Sruthán.

Cuing Ghnáis *(Custom's Yoke)*
An ember from the St John's Eve bonfire thrown in the field would, it was believed, bring luck to the crops and cattle.

Bile a Thit *(The Tree that Fell)*
Máirtín Ó Cadhain (1906-1970): The greatest writer of fiction in Irish and a perfervid fighter for Ireland and more especially its Irish-speaking communities.

Bile: an Irish word for a large tree, it has the connotation of sacredness and antiquity.

Meirge Mhurchú (Murchú's banner): At the battle of Clontarf in 1014 Brian Ború at morning, noon and evening asked his attendant how the battle fared. As long as his son Murchú's banner stood he knew the Irish would fight bravely, but when he asked the question for the third and last time, his attendant replied, 'The foreigners are now defeated, but the standard of Murchú has fallen.' 'Evil are those tidings', said the king, 'if Murchú is fallen the valour of the men of Erin is fled, and they shall never more look on a champion like him.'

Cionn tSáile (Kinsale): See note on *Mar Chaitheamar an Choinneal.*

Eachroim (Aughrim): known in Irish as *Eachroim an Áir* (Aughrim of the Slaughter) was the scene of the battle in 1691 where the Irish army under St Ruth was defeated by King William's troops under Ginkle. This battle, along with the Battle of the Boyne in 1690, was a fatal blow to what still survived of the Gaelic culture and language. It was followed by the Treaty of Limerick and the departure of Sarsfield and eleven thousand fighting men, representing most of the aristocracy of the nation, for France.

Scairbhsholais (Scarifhollis): The name means 'shallow ford of the light' and is a ford on the river Swilly, two miles west of Letterkenny, where the Cromwellian forces under Coote finally defeated the Ulster army in 1651. Coote ordered the slaughter of Owen Roe O'Neill's son Henry after the battle. Though resistance continued till 1652 it was a forlorn cause.

INDEX OF FIRST LINES

137